White Peak
Mountain Biking
The Pure Trails

VERTEBRATE **PUBLISHING**

Design and production by Vertebrate Publishing, Sheffield
www.**v-publishing**.co.uk

White Peak
MountainBiking
The Pure Trails

Written by
Jon Barton

Photography by **Andy Heading**

White Peak
MountainBiking
The Pure Trails

VG Copyright © 2006 Vertebrate Graphics Ltd

VP Published by **Vertebrate Publishing**

First printed 2006 Revised reprint 2009

ISBN 978-0-954-81314-7

Cover photo by **Andy Heading**: Fred Yong, dropping down Golf Course Hill, Bakewell.
Photography by **Andy Heading**.
Additional photography by **John Coefield** www.johncoefield.com.

Design & production by Nathan Ryder & Oliver Jackson.
Map illustrations by Nathan Ryder, Simon Norris & Oliver Jackson.
VERTEBRATE PUBLISHING   www.**v-graphics**.co.uk

Contents

ROUTE GRADES ▲ = MEDIUM ▲ = HARD ▲ = EXTREME (see page ix)

KEY TO THE MAP SYMBOLS

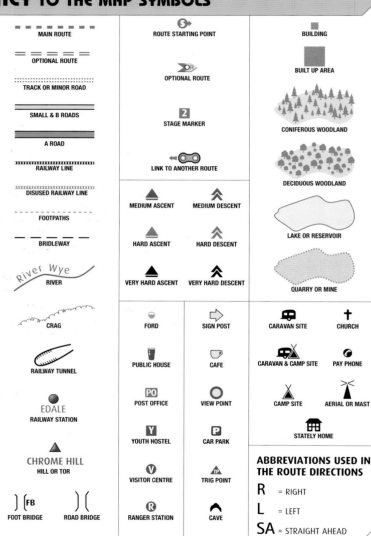

MAIN ROUTE

OPTIONAL ROUTE

TRACK OR MINOR ROAD

SMALL & B ROADS

A ROAD

RAILWAY LINE

DISUSED RAILWAY LINE

FOOTPATHS

BRIDLEWAY

River Wye
RIVER

CRAG

RAILWAY TUNNEL

EDALE
RAILWAY STATION

CHROME HILL
HILL OR TOR

FB
FOOT BRIDGE   **ROAD BRIDGE**

ROUTE STARTING POINT

OPTIONAL ROUTE

2
STAGE MARKER

LINK TO ANOTHER ROUTE

MEDIUM ASCENT   **MEDIUM DESCENT**

HARD ASCENT   **HARD DESCENT**

VERY HARD ASCENT   **VERY HARD DESCENT**

FORD   **SIGN POST**

PUBLIC HOUSE   **CAFE**

PO
POST OFFICE   **VIEW POINT**

Y
YOUTH HOSTEL   **P**
CAR PARK

V
VISITOR CENTRE   **TP**
TRIG POINT

R
RANGER STATION   **CAVE**

BUILDING

BUILT UP AREA

CONIFEROUS WOODLAND

DECIDUOUS WOODLAND

LAKE OR RESERVOIR

QUARRY OR MINE

CARAVAN SITE   **† CHURCH**

CARAVAN & CAMP SITE   **PAY PHONE**

CAMP SITE   **AERIAL OR MAST**

STATELY HOME

ABBREVIATIONS USED IN THE ROUTE DIRECTIONS

R = RIGHT

L = LEFT

SA = STRAIGHT AHEAD

Introduction

It would be a real shame if the White Peak, an area so full of potential, of deep valleys, high limestone hills and thick, leafy woodland, were not also full of legal trails. Happily enough, it's laced with them. Not only that, but they're some of the best trails in the country, the sort that leave you wondering: "Who built this, and if it were not specifically for mountain biking, then why?"

Whether you like to ride smoothly and delicately, flitting through the trees and over roots, or in a less subtle manner, being knocked sideways by a big block of limestone whilst pinballing downhill at mach thirty nine, there is a contender for your personal favourite piece of trail in the White Peak (I know everyone says this, but it's true, honestly!).

Although less well known than the more barren Dark Peak, the White Peak boasts some tremendous riding and, for some, its relatively unspoilt aspect is of great appeal. This guide picks up where its companion, *Dark Peak Mountain Biking – True Grit Trails* left off, describing all of the excellent biking in the southern half of the Peak District National Park, and also providing a little reminder of what's further north, in gritstone land.

The routes cover not only the limestone plateaux and dales, but all the idiosyncrasies of the area as well: the upper reaches of the River Dove and its rocky byways, the intricate singletrack traversing the open moorland of the Eastern Edges, and the magnificent vista of the River Wye, as it carves its way through the beds of limestone. It ventures upon the industrial relics of the Peak – the abandoned railway lines, viaducts, disused (and active quarries), mines and waterways.

The whole experience of compiling this volume has been very rewarding; it has been great getting to know the Peak in so much detail, seeing all of its landscape, wildlife and mountain bike action. What follows is the best of it. Enjoy.

As way of comparison, we've included a couple of new, excellent rides in the Dark Peak.

Jon Barton

Acknowledgements

A big "Thank You!" to all my riding companions over the years. In particular, thanks to everyone who has helped in compiling this book. Andy Heading has been a great inspiration, not only a superb snapper but a great source of route info, local knowledge and general support. Thanks also to the hard working team at Vertebrate for their second-to-none efforts in production, Nathan Ryder for his excellent design skills – day and night! – and Tom Fenton, for being editor in chief and filling in all the gaps that his rather hurried author left out. And of course Simon Norris, for *a)* having the faith to approve the project and *b)* getting the maps drawn with Nathan. Further more, thanks to our hard working distributor Cordee for their support and encouragement, and to Paul Evans, for all his ground-breaking work on *Dark Peak Mountain Biking* which paved the way for this volume. Thanks also to Nick Cotton for his excellent *Traffic Free Cycling* book, the inspiration for our 'Family Rides' section. Thanks to the photographic models – sorry if it didn't turn out to be quite as glamourous as we promised – you did say you were up for some dirty pictures, thanks to Jane and Julian Winstanley, Fred Yong and Ben Eagle. And finally thanks to Gráinne and of course Thomas James – whose feet at last reach the pedals.

How to Use This Book

This book should provide you with all of the information that you need for an enjoyable, trouble-free and successful ride. The following tips should also be of help:

1. We strongly recommend that you invest in some of the following maps: *Ordnance Survey Explorer® OL24 (1:25,000) The Peak District, White Peak Area*; *Ordnance Survey Explorer® OL1 (1:25,000) The Peak District, Dark Peak Area,* and *Harvey Superwalker Dark Peak* map. These are essential, even if you are familiar with the area – you may need to cut the ride short or take an alternative route.

2. Choose your route. Consider the time you have available and the ability/level of experience of each member of your party – then read the safety section of this guide.

3. We recommend that you study the route description carefully before setting off. Cross-reference this to your map so that you've got a good sense of general orientation in case you need an escape route. Make sure that you are familiar with the symbols used on the maps.

The routes

This guide contains 26 of the best routes in the southern half of the Peak District, with a few new Dark Peak routes thrown in for good measure. Some of the rides are just as good in reverse and many get better on the second and third ride as you learn the best bits.

Classics are fairly short (but not necessarily easy). **Epics** are a little longer and require that bit more effort and **Enduros** step things up again.

Grades

Routes, climbs and descents are graded blue, red and black, in a similar system to that used at many of the trail centres around the UK.

▲ = Easy   ▲ = Moderate   ▲ = Hard

The grades are based on average conditions – good weather and not too wet and muddy. In a drought the routes will feel easier, in the depths of winter, harder. Grades consider technicality, length, climbs, navigation, and remoteness – so one 'black' route might be a short all-out technical test while another could be a big endurance challenge with tricky navigation. As ever, these grades are subjective. How you find a particular route, downhill or climb will be dictated by your own levels of fitness and skill.

Directions & Accuracy

While every effort has been made to ensure accuracy within the directions in this guide, things change and we are unable to guarantee that every detail will be correct. Please treat stated distances as guidelines. **Please exercise caution if a direction appears at odds with the route on the ground. A comparison between direction and map should see you on the right track.**

Rights of Way

Countryside access in the UK hasn't been particularly kind to cyclists, although things are improving. We have 'right of way' on bridleways (blue arrows on signs) and byways (red arrows). However, having 'right of way' doesn't actually mean having the right of way, just that we're allowed to ride there – so give way to walkers and horse riders. We're also allowed to ride on green lanes and some unclassified roads, although the only way to determine which are legal and which aren't is to check with the local countryside authority. Obviously, cycle routes are also in.

The very understanding Forestry Commission generally allows cyclists to use its land (again, you'll need to check with them first to be sure). You must, however, obey all signs, especially those warning of forestry operations – a fully loaded logging truck will do more than scuff your frame...

Everything else is out of bounds (unless, of course, the landowner says otherwise). Riding illegally can upset walkers, (who have every right to enjoy their day); is, in many cases, technically classed as trespass (meaning you could be prosecuted for any damage caused). **Please don't do it**.

Not all tracks are signed, so it's not always obvious whether that great-looking trail you want to follow is an illegal footpath or a legal bridleway. That's why it's a good idea to carry a map with you on every ride.

The Bike

Any half-decent mountain bike will be fine (try and avoid a '£99 special'). A full suspension bike will add comfort and control. A lightweight race number will make hills easier and something with a bit of travel will help on technical descents. We'd pick a compromise somewhere between the three, depending on your personal preferences.

Check everything's working – you won't be going uphill fast if your gears seize but equally you'll be a little quicker than planned if your brakes fail coming down. Pump the tyres up, check nothing's about to wear through and make sure that everything that should be tight is tight.

Essential Kit

Helmet
"The best helmet is the one that you're wearing". Make sure it fits, you're wearing it correctly and that it won't move in a crash.

Clothing
You need to get your clothing right if you want to stay comfortable on a bike, especially in bad weather. The easiest way to do this is to follow a layering system. Begin with clothing made from 'technical' synthetic or wool fabrics that will wick the sweat away from your body and then dry quickly, keeping you dry and warm. Stay away from cotton – it absorbs moisture and holds onto it. If it's chilly, an insulating layer will keep you warm, and a wind/waterproof layer on the outside protects from the elements. Layers can then be removed or added to suit the conditions. Padded shorts are more comfortable, but the amount of lycra on display is down to you. Baggy shorts, full length tights and trousers are all available to match the conditions. Set off a little on the cold side – you'll soon warm up. Don't leave the warm clothes behind though, as the weather can turn quickly.

Gloves
Gloves ward off blisters and numb hands and help keep your fingers warm. They also provide a surprising amount of protection when you come off.

Footwear
Flat pedals/clips-ins – it's your call. Make sure you can walk in the shoes and that they have sufficient tread for you to do so. Consider overshoes if it's chilly.

Other essentials
As mentioned, take any necessary spares, tools, tube and pump, spare clothes, first aid kit, food and water. Stop short of the kitchen sink, as you'll still want to be able to actually ride your bike.

You'll need something to carry this lot in. We'd suggest a hydration pack, as they allow you to drink on the move and keep excess weight off the bike.

Night Riding

Night riding is ace! It's possible to enjoy an after-work ride in the depths of winter in your favourite off-road playground. But it's a completely different ball game and (hardly surprisingly) there are a few risks to be aware of.

Lights and batteries

Invest carefully in a lighting system. Consider battery life, weight, number/type of bulbs and power. Fully charge your battery before a ride (sounds like common sense, until you forget). Carry a secondary light source (such as a head torch) for emergencies (it's surprising what you can ride with a commuter light if you have to, although it isn't much fun). Pack a rear light for road sections and keep it clean.

Route planning and safety

Choose your ride on the basis of battery life. Time it yourself, don't necessarily rely on the manufacturer's information. Allow extra time – you'll be slower in the dark. Stay on ground that you are familiar with at first (night-time navigation in unfamiliar territory demands military expertise) and not too far from home. Ride with a friend. Watch out for the werewolves. Tell someone you're out. **Ride within your limits – trees loom up very quickly in the dark!**

General Safety

The ability to read a map, navigate in poor visibility and to understand weather warnings is essential. Don't head out in bad weather, unless you're confident and capable of doing so.

Some of the routes described point you at tough climbs and steep descents that can potentially be very dangerous. Too much exuberance on a steep descent in the middle of nowhere and you could be in more than a spot of bother, especially if you're alone. Consider your limitations and relative fragility.

Be self-sufficient. Carry food and water, spares, a tube and a pump. Consider a first-aid kit. Even if it's warm, the weather could turn, so take a wind/waterproof. Think about what could happen on an enforced stop. Pack lights if you could finish in the dark.

If you're riding solo, think about the seriousness of an accident – you might be without help for a very long time. Tell someone where you're going, when you'll be back and tell them once you are back. Take a mobile phone if you have one, but don't expect a signal. And **don't** call out the ambulance because you've grazed your knee.

Riding in a group is safer (ambitious overtaking manoeuvres excepted) and often more fun, but don't leave slower riders too far behind and give them a minute for a breather when they've caught up. Allow extra time for a group ride, as you'll inevitably stop and chat. You might need an extra top if you're standing around for a while. Ride within your ability, make sure you can slow down fast and give way to other users. Bells might be annoying, but they work. If you can't bring yourself to bolt one on, a polite 'excuse me' should be fine. **On hot, sunny days, slap on some Factor 30+ and** ALWAYS WEAR YOUR HELMET!

In the Event of an Accident

In the event of an accident requiring immediate assistance: Dial **999** and ask for POLICE or AMBULANCE. If you can supply the services with a grid reference of exactly where you are it should help to speed up their response time.

Rules of the (Off) Road

1. Always ride on legal trails.
2. Ride considerately – give way to horses and pedestrians.
3. Don't spook animals.
4. Ride in control – you don't know who's around the next corner.
5. Leave gates as you find them – if you're unsure, shut them.
6. Keep the noise down and don't swear loudly when you fall off in front of walkers.
7. Leave no trace – take home everything you took out.
8. Keep water sources clean – don't take toilet stops near streams.
9. Enjoy the countryside and respect its life and work.

Planning Your Ride

1. Consider the ability/experience of each rider in your group. Check the weather forecast. How much time do you have available? Now choose your route.
2. Study the route description before setting off, and cross-reference it with the relevant map.
3. Bear in mind everything we've suggested about safety, clothing, spares and food and drink.
4. Get out there and get dirty.

Thanks to:

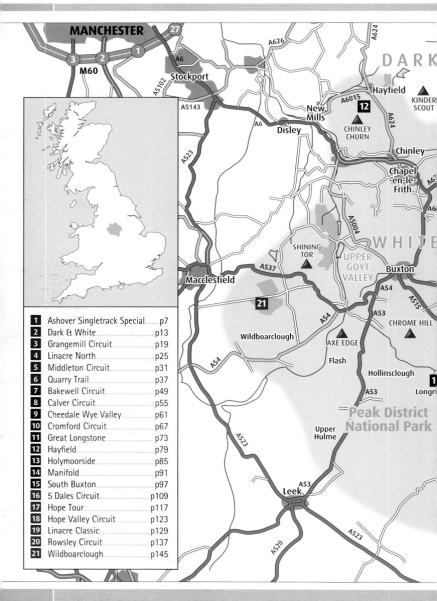

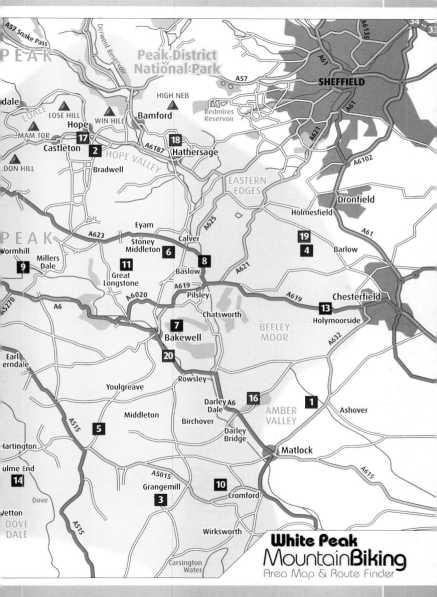

SECTION 1

Classics

A quick blast after work, a night loop you can finish before your lights run out, or a ride to squeeze in when you're short of time and energy. That's a classic. Relatively low on distance and never taking you too far from home, these are still good, solid rides – kind of like Fawlty Towers – highly entertaining, but not running for too long.

Classics sponsored by

GORE
BIKE·WEAR

www.gorebikewear.com

CLASSIC TRAILS ABOVE ASHOVER VILLAGE

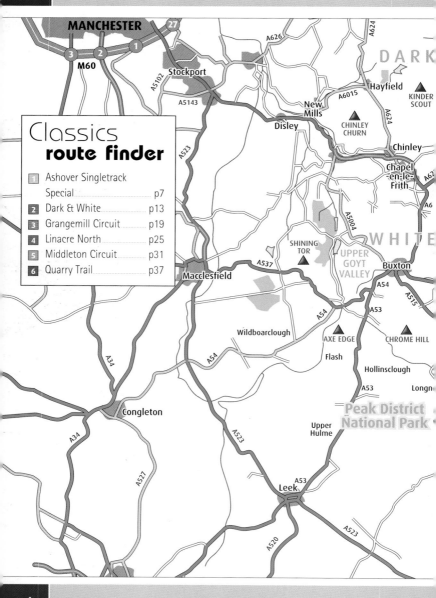

MANCHESTER

M60

Stockport

A626

A5102

A5143

A6015

Hayfield

KINDER SCOUT

New Mills

Disley

CHINLEY CHURN

Chinley

Chapel-en-le-Frith

DARK

A624

A624

A67

A6

A523

SHINING TOR

A5004

WHITE

UPPER GOYT VALLEY

Buxton

Macclesfield

A537

A54

A54

A53

A515

Wildboarclough

AXE EDGE

CHROME HILL

Flash

Hollinsclough

Longn

A34

A54

A53

Peak District National Park

Congleton

A523

Upper Hulme

A34

A527

A53

Leek

A523

A520

Classics Route Finder

CLIMBING ABOVE THE RAVENSNEST

Ashover Singletrack Special – E.Peak 11km

Introduction

A fantastic ride, mainly on singletrack, with some good descents and one of the hardest climbs in this guide. Although short, it is a test of your mountain bike skills, with technical river crossings, the odd obstacle and sustained ups and downs. Oddly enough it makes an ideal test track for a new bike or bit of kit – as it has a bit of everything, but is not too far to push home should the kit not live up to expectations. Like a lot of the White Peak, the best time to ride the trail is in late summer when it is dry, and the vegetation is dying back.

The Ride

Tracing a loop around the Amber Valley, starting from the village of Ashover, the ride crosses the river and kicks straight in with a big climb. Fantastic singletrack and another, more amenable climb then leads to some quiet lanes which once again perch the rider on the lip of the Amber Valley, before another great descent and a final bit of trail leads back to Ashover.

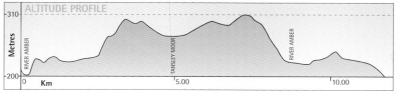

ASHOVER SINGLETRACK SPECIAL   **GRADE:** ▲

DISTANCE: 11KM
START/FINISH: ASHOVER VILLAGE
PARKING: ON-STREET PARKING IN ASHOVER VILLAGE
PUBLIC HOUSE: OLD POETS' CORNER, ASHOVER Tel: 01246 590 888

TOTAL ASCENT: 350M
GRID REFERENCE: SK 349633
CAFÉ: SANDWICH TIME

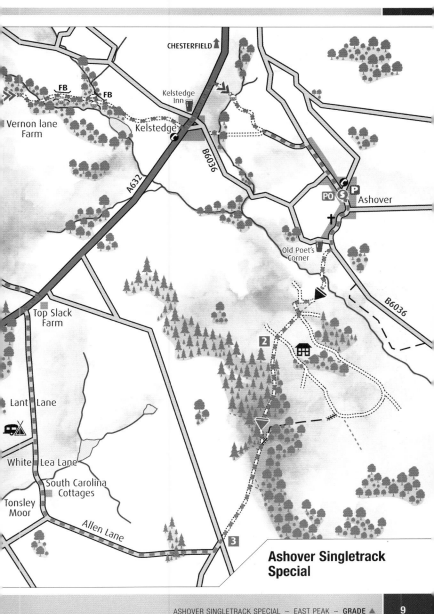

Ashover Singletrack Special

Directions – Ashover Singletrack Special

⑤ Head downhill from the parking, past the church towards the T-junction. Turn **L** and take the bridleway **R**, down the side of the pub. Descend to the river, and then dig deep for a very tough climb – thankfully short lived. After the climb, the bridleway meets a track. Turn **L** along this track and after 50m, **R**, arriving at a crossroads after a further 100m.

2 Go **SA** onto a bridleway (more stone slab surface) and head off up into the woods, pleasant climbing, to emerge in the open at old quarry workings. (Have a play on the tracks if you fancy.) Keep **SA** uphill, ignore the **L** fork heading down, and a final steep push gains tarmac and the road.

3 **SA** at this crossroads taking Allen Lane, **R** after 75m. Follow this **SA**, taking the first **R**, past South Carolina Cottages, on Whitelea Lane. Keep **SA** onto Lant Lane, to meet the busy road. Turn **R** and first **L**. Head along this road, watch out for motorbikes doing 150mph and take the first **R** after 750m. Pass a car park and then take the farm track signed to Vernon Lane Farm.

4 Descend to the farm, take the path forking **L** at the gates, and follow this fantastic technical descent to the river, ford it (at your peril) or use the bridge. The second ford is a little less deep; follow the trail into the hamlet of Kelstedge. At the main road turn **L**, uphill, and after the last house (farm) take the broad track **R**, this soon improves into more singletrack and drops one with interest back to the road, turn **R** at the T-junction back into Ashover.

◀━☉☉ Making a day of it

Why not make a 'night' of it as well? This isn't a bad little route to do in the dark – with lights, of course.

FAST DESCENT ON BRADWELL HILL

Dark & White – Central Peak   13.75km

Introduction

This is a full-on mountain bike route, sampling typical white and dark terrain, with challenging climbs and descents on both gritstone and limestone. Although the route has fine views, you won't notice them, as you will be pedalling hard on the climbs, or hanging in on the descents.

The Ride

From the Peak mountain bike capital of Hope, the route heads up Edale, before climbing the rocky lane onto the side of Win Hill known as Hope Brink. A fantastic descent speeds down to the hamlet of Aston, and then across the valley floor to Brough. Well warmed up, fit and skillful cyclists will style the steep rocky climb of Brough Lane before descending to Bradwell. With a steady cooling-down to pass the cement works you'll make it back to Hope in time for tea.

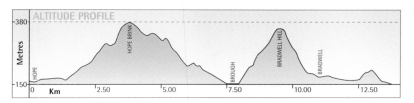

ALTITUDE PROFILE

Metres: 380 ... 150

Km: 0 — 2.50 — 5.00 — 7.50 — 10.00 — 12.50

(Labels on profile: HOPE, HOPE BRINK, BROUGH, BRADWELL HILL, BRADWELL)

DARK & WHITE   GRADE: ▲

DISTANCE: 13.75KM
START/FINISH: HOPE
PARKING: PAY AND DISPLAY, HOPE VILLAGE
PUBLIC HOUSE: PLENTY TO CHOOSE FROM IN HOPE

TOTAL ASCENT: 530M
GRID REFERENCE: SK 171835
CAFÉ: WOODBINE CAFÉ, HOPE Tel: 07778 113 882

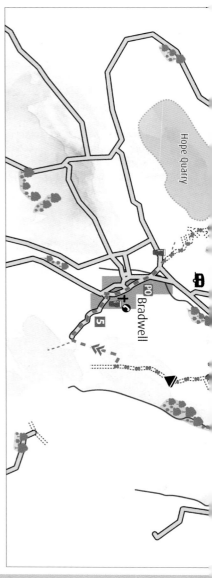

Hope Quarry

PO

Bradwell

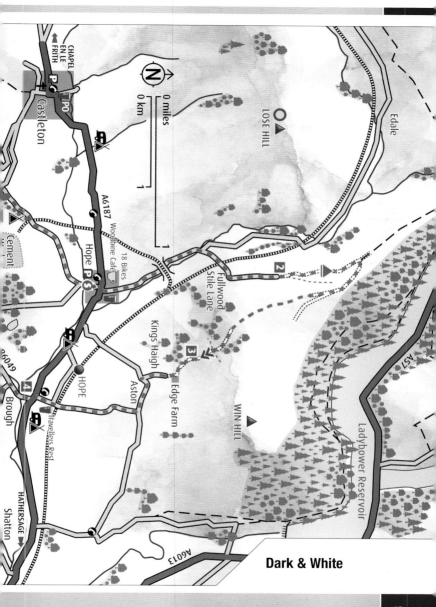

Dark & White

Directions – Dark & White

❺▶ From the pay and display car park on the main road in *Hope*, leave the car park, turning **R**, and take the first **L**, signposted *Edale*, on Edale Road. Follow this road for just over 1km, going **SA** up Fullwood Stile Lane, just after crossing the river by the bridge on the bend. Up the lane, swing **L** and steadily climb on worsening tarmac to a gate.

2 **SA** up the rocky lane, all very rideable for the determined. It soon levels off. Splash through the puddles, and a final sharp climb leads up to a junction by the gate. Turn back **R**, (don't go through the gate) and follow the trail uphill, looking out for a small cairn after 750m, (if you reach another gate you have overshot). Fork **R** at the cairn, heading downhill on the fine trail.

3 Continue through a couple of gates, bearing **R** across the grassy field, heading for the muddy lane at the left side of the woods. Down the lane, through a couple of gates to reach tarmac at Edge Farm. Downhill to the junction. Turn **L** and at the summit of the second dip, turn **R** downhill on good fast tarmac, to soon reach the main road.

4 Turn **L** to the traffic lights, then **R** onto Brough Lane End, over the bridge, turning **L** up Brough Lane. Follow steepening tarmac up and then round to the **R**, uphill to where it becomes a rocky lane and turns nasty. Persevere, as it eases once around the shallow rightward bend, where steady climbing leads up to a signed bridleway through a gate to the **R**. Take this across the field then head **L** downhill, onto the fast singletrack descent (watch the gate!), dropping down to the village of Bradwell.

5 Head downhill into the village, and onto the main road. Turn **R**. Through the traffic lights and **SA** taking the **L** turn of Town Lane, just before the small football field, keep **SA** onto a signed bridleway which weaves its way through the cement works, to eventually emerge onto a tarmac road. Turn **R** and follow the road back into the village of Hope. Turn **L** to the car park.

◀️●◉●◇ **Making a day of it**

The circuit can be extended neatly into the **Hope Tour** loop (see page 117). From the most northerly point on the circuit (**GR SK 165868**), pick up the **Hope Tour** and follow that round into Aston (**GR SK 185839**) where you can rejoin the original ride.

Grangemill – South Peak

Introduction

A good circuit to do when the rest of the Peak is sitting under a veil of mud. With plenty of fast sections, and limited opportunity for mud to form, this circuit is a good winter trip, or indeed a good beginners ride. For a long and fast ride, link it with the Middleton Circuit, fit your semi-slicks and see how quickly you can do it.

The Ride

Starting off with a blast along the High Peak Trail, the ride cuts off across country, mostly on good tracks, with a field or two, before dropping into Grangemill. Pleasant lanes gain height again, with a section of farm track leading you back to the start to complete the circuit.

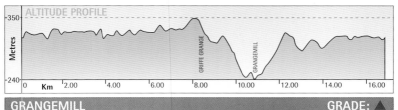

GRANGEMILL   **GRADE:** ▲

DISTANCE: 17KM

START/FINISH: PLANTATION (HIGH PEAK TRAIL)

PARKING: FREE CAR PARK ON HIGH PEAK TRAIL

TOTAL ASCENT: 366M

GRID REFERENCE: SK 195582

CAFÉ: BRING SANDWICHES

PUBLIC HOUSE: HOLLY BUSH INN, GRANGEMILL Tel: 01629 650 300

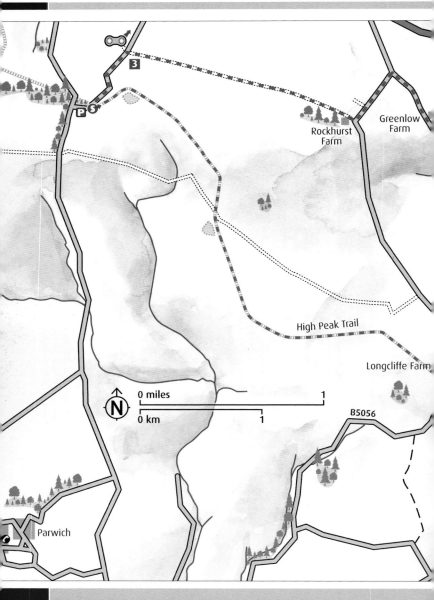

Grangemill

Directions – Grangemill

↱ Leave the car park and head east on the High Peak Trail. Follow this disused railway track for approximately 8km, looking out for Harboro Rocks on the left – a kind of mini Dolomites. 1km further on, the trail starts to run parallel to a road and after 100 metres, turn **L** on the signed bridleway to *Grangemill Head* across the field. Over some stiles by gates and the trail soon becomes a track. Go **SA** where the track swings left, down a fine fast bridleway to join a larger track. Follow this turning **L**, then downhill, ignoring a leftwards branch up to a farm, down then back up, through some gates, looking out for signed bridleway to *Grangemill* on the **R**. Take this (good singletrack) down through the cow field to the crossroads, pub and hubbub of Grangemill.

2 Take the road **L** towards Longcliffe, but after 150m turn **R** up a narrow lane towards Aldwark. Head uphill and go **SA** through the village, taking the lane to the **L** after approximately 1.5km. Follow this lane for 300m, to where it swings **L**, at Rockhurst Farm. At this point take the farm track, off to the **R** and follow this to the road.

3 Turn **L** and head back along the lane to the car park.

⊸◯⊃ **Making a day of it**

At its west end, the **Grangemill Circuit** briefly joins the **Middleton Circuit** (see page 31) on a lane near Gotham (**GR SK 198586**). In the east, it meets the **Cromford** loop (see page 67) in Grangemill itself (**GR SK 243576**). Just thought we'd let you know...

ON THE HIGH PEAK TRAIL

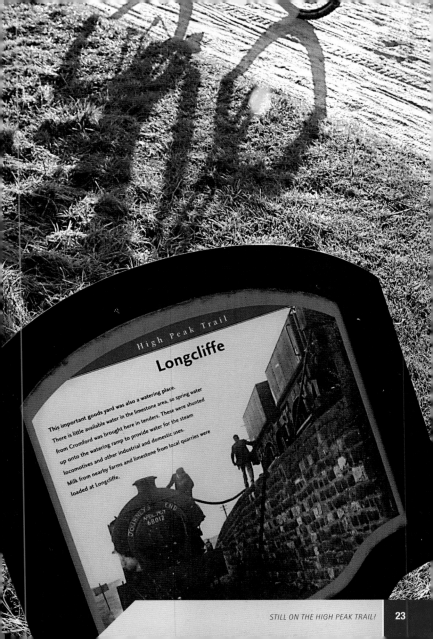

High Peak Trail

Longcliffe

This important goods yard was also a watering place.
There is little available water in the limestone area, so spring water
from Cromford was brought here in tenders. These were shunted
up onto the watering ramp to provide water for the steam
locomotives and other industrial and domestic uses.
Milk from nearby farms and limestone from local quarries were
loaded at Longcliffe.

Linacre North – East Peak

23km

Introduction

A sister to Holymoorside, and an obvious choice to combine with that route for a good day out. Plenty of singletrack and mud in the off-season, make this a real 'love or hate' ride, depending on the conditions.

The Ride

Heading south from the reservoir, through the village of Old Brampton, fast tracks and slow hills lead round to Wigley, from where a superb descent leads to a tough little climb north to Birley. The ride continues north making its way up hill and down dale on a variety of tracks and singletrack trails into the village of Holmesfield. The downhill leg is just that, with most of the ups done on the road, leaving fast trails to test the concentration, down to Barlow, on to Cutthorpe and so back to the reservoirs.

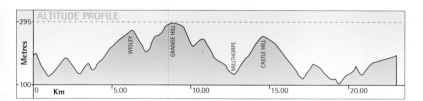

LINACRE NORTH   GRADE: ▲

DISTANCE: 23KM

START/FINISH: LINACRE RESERVOIRS

PARKING: FREE CAR PARK

TOTAL ASCENT: 693M

GRID REFERENCE: SK 334729

CAFÉ: ICE CREAM VAN AT THE CAR PARK ON NICE DAYS

PUBLIC HOUSE: THE PEACOCK INN, CUTTHORPE Tel: 02146 232 834

B6050

Farm

GRANGE HILL

4

Birley Farm

B6050

Wigley Hall Farm

Royal Oak

3

A619

The Gate Inn

N

0 miles

0 km

Linacre Reservoir

P

P R

George & Dragon

Old Brampton

2

The Peacock Inn

Cutthorpe

the Three Merry Lads

Linacre North

Directions – Linacre North

5 Turn **R** out of the car park (first parking bay on right as you head down the lane from the main road) and head downhill into the woods, going **SA** as you pass the ranger station on the left. Take the bridleway uphill coming in at an acute angle from the **R** (just after the bridge) and head up through the trees and out into the open, to eventually meet a road. Turn **L** and head down the road a short distance to take a bridleway on the **R**.

2 Descend to the stream and take the track **R** at the next T-junction, follow this uphill, turning **R** back downhill, where the track turns to tarmac. Follow this, past the farm and onwards and uphill to meet the road.

3 Turn **L** and take the next **R** signposted to *Wigley*, follow the lane and bear **L** down the bridleway by the stone toadstool. Twisty, rooty exciting descent leads to the stream, cross this and climb back out up to Birley Farm as the path turns to a mown strip of grass, then head **L** along the tarmac lane, through the fine gates.

4 **R** opposite the pond and through a gate onto a bridleway into the trees. Follow this **SA** onto a track and up the hill towards the road, staying left at the farm. Turn **L** onto the road and second **R** at the junction. After approximately 1km take a track on the **R** down to Grange Lumb Farm. Go past the farm and down **L** into the trees, cross the stream, heading out the other side to emerge onto a tarmac farm track and head uphill to the road.

5 **L** and after a couple of hundred metres take the bridleway off to the **R**, all good solid downhill fun to emerge onto Johnnygate Lane. Look out for a bridleway off to the **L** by some houses; take this to descend over a couple of fords into the village of Milnthorpe. Go more or less **SA** over the road onto Milnthorpe Lane, and after 150m take the muddy bridleway off to the **L**, by the bus stop. Tough, it just gets tougher, climbing towards the source of the Amazon with a ▶OR▶ cop-out track on the **R** which heads up to the road, if you need it. Turn **R** into Holmesfield.

6 Turn **R** at the T-junction and head through the village, past the pub and church to take the first **R** down to Cartledge. Take the bridleway **L** in the centre of the hamlet and it's downhill for a couple of kilometres to the road. Turn **L**, downhill, keep **SA** at the junction, climbing up, and up, taking the first road to the **R** for a steep road climb, before descending for nearly 1km. Take the bridleway **R**, where the road turns sharp left, i.e. at the T-junction.

7 Follow Gateland Lane down to the river. Cross this, keeping **SA** for a stiff little climb/ push up to the road, uphill then **SA** on the road into Barlow. Take the first **R** up Wilkin Hill, looking out for a bridleway off to the **L** a couple of hundred metres past the junction. Take this down to the stream, **SA** up the hill and back up to join Common Lane and so into Cutthorpe village. Turn **R** and head up the road for just over 1km, turning **L** down to the starting car park, and the reservoirs.

◀━◯◯ Making a day of it

Same start and finish point as **Holymoorside** (see page 85). Combine the two for a big ride – which will probably feel twice the size in the winter mud, but brilliant on the dry summer trails.

JONNIE B ON JOHNNYGATE

Middleton Circuit – South Peak

Introduction

A companion to the Grangemill Circuit. When combined, the two make a brilliant ride, taking in quintessential White Peak scenery. This route is a bolder proposition than the Grangemill Circuit; still a reliable option for the winter, but with more 'real' mountain biking.

The Ride

The route warms up along a quiet lane, then drops into Long Dale, which was once a glacial spillway. Climb out and drop down to Middleton, not quite a remnant from the last ice age, but certainly maintaining much olde worlde charm. It is all good fast lanes and well-surfaced disused railways back to the start, but with enough hills to keep the legs interested.

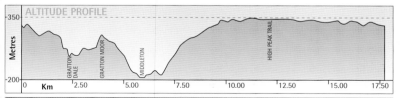

MIDDLETON	**GRADE:** ▲
DISTANCE: 17.5KM	**TOTAL ASCENT:** 344M
START/FINISH: PLANTATION (HIGH PEAK TRAIL)	**GRID REFERENCE:** SK 195582
PARKING: FREE CAR PARK ON TRAIL	**CAFÉ:** JUST OFF ROUTE, ELTON CAFÉ, ELTON Tel: 01629 650 217
PUBLIC HOUSE: UP THE ROAD TO YOULGREAVE: THE FARMYARD INN, YOULGREAVE Tel: 01629 636 221	

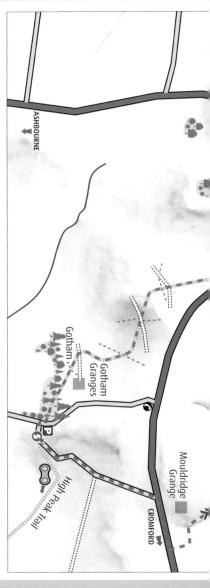

ASHBOURNE

Gotham

Gotham
Granges

P

High peak trail

Mouldridge
Grange

CROMFORD

Middleton Circuit

Directions – Middleton Circuit

➤ From the car park, go back onto the road and turn **L**, heading up what is Mouldridge Lane, soon joining the main A5012. Turn **R** and follow the road for 300m, taking the bridleway off to the **L**. Follow this as it becomes a great little descent into Long Dale. Keep **L** where the trail splits, heading up the floor of Long Dale. Easy going becomes hard going as the trail starts to climb up and out of the dale. Where the track levels off, head **R** over to the wall.

2 Go through the gate and onto a more distinct track. Follow this, through more gates, looking out for a singletrack branching off **L** as the track swings round to the **R**. Take this narrow bridleway and emerging onto the road, keep **SA** into the village of Middleton.

3 **L** at the crossroads, climbing steeply uphill, taking the **L** fork, still on tarmac, after approximately 300m. Follow this – Whitfield Lane, soon deteriorating into rough track. Drop downhill to a T-junction, just in front of a large house, head **R**, not **L** – that only leads to Mount Pleasant Farm.

4 Follow the track to where it meets the road and turn **R** for 800m up to the cross roads, turn **L** along the track; keep **SA** on Green Lane, to where it crosses the High Peak Trail. Turn **L** onto the High Peak Trail. Follow the excellent and fast disused railway line back (after about 5km) to the car park.

◄⊙⊃ **Making a day of it**

The **Middleton Circuit** briefly joins the **Grangemill Circuit** (see page 19) on a lane near Gotham (GR SK **198586**). Join the two for a big old ride. Alternatively, it runs along the High Peak Trail for a short way. Not in any way technical, but a nice way to see the sights and get some miles in, this can be followed in either direction for as long as your legs will carry you.

The Quarry Trail – Central Peak

11.5km

Introduction

The Peak District National Park is a very busy place; there is a balancing act between tourists, recreational users, agriculture and industry. This short ride gives a flavour of everything that the Peak stands for. Essentially a circuit of several huge quarries, it also takes in the twee village of Eyam, with its doilied tea rooms, the rough and tumble of proper mountain biking on the high farming pastures of Middleton Moor, and of course mineral and limestone workings galore. This route is ideal as an introduction to mountain biking and a great night ride.

The Ride

Starting from the large lay-by-cum-car park at the western end of Stoney Middleton, just past and opposite the Lovers Leap Bistro, the ride heads down the dale, before traversing the Great Longstone Edge ridge, following a vein of fluorspar. The route then briefly leaves the quarry-scape behind, crossing the delightful Coombs Dale. It climbs back up then descends fast back to Stoney Dale before a final loop around Eyam drops you rapidly back to Stoney Middleton.

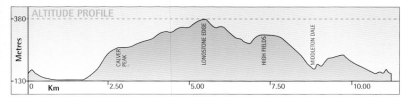

ALTITUDE PROFILE

Metres

CALVER PEAK · LONGSTONE EDGE · HIGH FIELDS · MIDDLETON DALE

380

130

0   Km   2.50   5.00   7.50   10.00

THE QUARRY TRAIL   GRADE: ▲

DISTANCE: 11.5KM
START/FINISH: STONEY MIDDLETON
PARKING: LAY-BY ON A623, 50m WEST OF THE LOVERS LEAP BISTRO
PUBLIC HOUSE: THE MOON, STONEY MIDDLETON Tel: 01433 630 203
TOTAL ASCENT: 450M
GRID REFERENCE: SK 227757
CAFÉ: OUTSIDE, CALVER CROSSROADS Tel: 01433 631 111

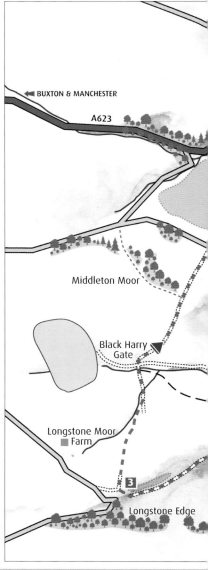

BUXTON & MANCHESTER

A623

Middleton Moor

Black Harry
Gate

Longstone Moor
Farm

3

Longstone Edge

The Quarry Trail

Directions – The Quarry Trail

➤ **R** out of lay-by, downhill on the A623 through the village of Stoney Middleton, down to the traffic lights at Calver crossroads, ignoring the excellent café in *Outside* – it's not time for a stop yet. Turn **R** and head uphill for 400m taking the gated farm track up **R**, just after the end of the houses.

2 The track zig-zags up, and up and up, eventually levelling out, where you take the **L** fork. Continue on to a crossroads, turn **R** and keep to the good track, **ignore** the tracks leading left and watch out for the big hole on your left. Keep **SA** on the main track, with huge quarry workings to your right, as the path undulates for nearly 3km.

3 Turn **R** onto a bridleway at the end of the quarries, just before a *Give Way* sign and prior to the road becoming good tarmac. Go through the gate and turn immediately **L** through another gate then **R** and head along the track keeping the wall to your right. Good fast singletrack and faint paths lead **SA** down to Black Harry's Gate, at the head of Coombs Dale. Continue **SA** up the gritty rutted short climb, over the brow **SA** over the tarmac road and fast down past yet more quarries to emerge, brakes permitting, slowly on to the busy *A623*.

4 Go more or less **SA** across the road and up the minor road to Eyam, steady road climbing leading into the village. Take the first **R**, Lydgate, follow this to where the tarmac path forks either side of a row of houses. Take the **L** fork, through the gate and a good fast sweeping descent all too soon leads you into the maze of back streets of Stoney. Follow your nose back onto the main road, turn **R** and back up to the lay-by on the left after 200m.

◄⊂⊙⊃ **Making a day of it**

Roll down the road to Calver (**GR SK 239748**) and pick up the **Calver Circuit** (see page 55). Follow it in reverse until you meet the **Great Longstone** ride (see page 73) near Rowland (**GR SK 213721**). Reverse this and return to the **Quarry Trail** at Black Harry Gate (**GR SK 206743**).

SECTION 2

Epics

Getting longer now – these loops will take a bit more time and effort. Not rides to be sacred of, but definitely rides to be respected. Rather large hills and plenty of technical ground to cover mean that firstly, you're going to be out for a good few hours and secondly, you're going to have a really good time.

Epics

sponsored by **bike**magic.com

www.bikemagic.com

DROPPING INTO THE CHATSWORTH ESTATE PHOTO: JOHN COEFIELD

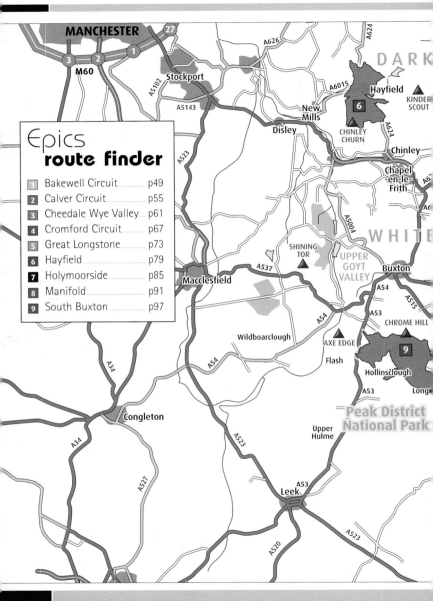

MANCHESTER

M60

Stockport

New Mills

Disley

DARK

Hayfield

KINDER SCOUT

6

CHINLEY CHURN

Chinley

Chapel-en-le-Frith

WHITE

SHINING TOR

UPPER GOYT VALLEY

Buxton

Macclesfield

Wildboarclough

AXE EDGE

Flash

CHROME HILL

9

Hollinsclough

Long

Congleton

Upper Hulme

Peak District National Park

Leek

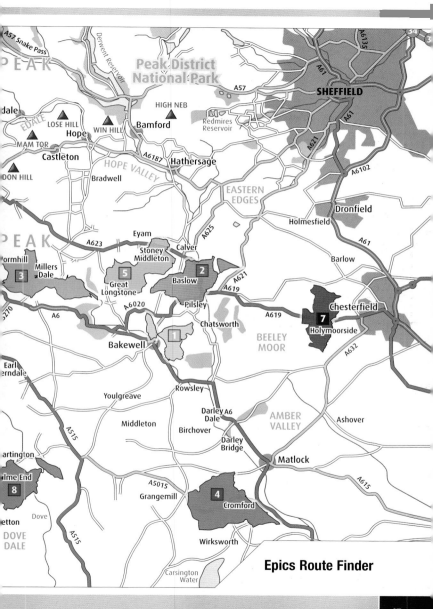

Epics Route Finder

CALTON PASTURES PHOTO: JOHN COEFIELD

Bakewell Circuit – Central Peak

Introduction

Tea rooms, a country house, a golf course and quaint stone footbridges over well-stocked trout streams are no indication of the absolute hardcore fast paced XC riding that this circuit offers. Some of the best woodland singletrack, a dollop of up and a dollop of down – enjoy.

This ride has been designed to be as close to a perfect mini enduro lap as we could get it. It is ideal for both the newcomer to mountain biking wanting to know what all the fuss is really about, or for the seasoned pro, wanting an excellent spin out. A competent rider should get round this non-stop, no foot-downs.

The Ride

We start with a reminder of what we are escaping from, but we soon leave the congestion of town and road for a brisk climb over Cracknowl Hill. Next comes a warm-up along the disused railway track of the Monsal Trail. The rest of the ride is a combination of fast tracks, big aerobic climbs, super-fast grassy descents and of course the fantastic Golf Course Hill descent into Bakewell.

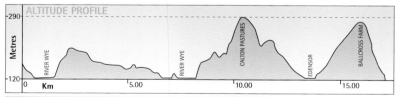

ALTITUDE PROFILE

Metres — 290, 120 | Km: 0, 5.00, 10.00, 15.00

RIVER WYE · RIVER WYE · CALTON PASTURES · EDENSOR · BALLCROSS FARM

BAKEWELL CIRCUIT **GRADE:** ▲

DISTANCE: 17KM

START/FINISH: BAKEWELL

PARKING: LARGE PAY AND DISPLAY

PUBLIC HOUSE: PLENTY TO CHOOSE FROM IN BAKEWELL

TOTAL ASCENT: 550M

GRID REFERENCE: SK 220686

CAFÉ: THE BAKEWELL PUDDING PARLOUR Tel: 01629 815 107

CHESTERFIELD

B6048

B5020

Chatsworth
House

Edensor

PO

Edensor
Tea Rooms

Ball Cross
Farm

6

5

B6012

Bakewell
Golf
Course

Calton Pastures

Calton Houses

Monsal Trail

4

Haddon Park
Farm

3

Haddon Park

Bakewell Circuit

MATLOCK

0 miles   1

0 km   1

Directions – Bakewell Circuit

➊ Exiting the main Bakewell car park, turn **L** and queue with the traffic over the bridge, to the roundabout and head **SA** on the A6 signed *Buxton*. After 500m turn **R** just by the speed camera, across a stone footbridge, go **SA** up the track under the old bridge. Climb steadily uphill, taking the **R** fork at the junction. The track levels off then drops down to the Monsal Trail.

➋ Turn **R** and follow the trail, rapidly weaving in and out of the prams and pedestrians to its end, some 3km later. Turn off the trail, **ignore** the tarmac and drop down into the fields towards the river. Follow the bridleway as it weaves along the valley floor, before exiting onto a metalled road. Curve **L** up the road, over the tunnel entrance, watching out for a gate and bridleway off to the **R**, into the field.

➌ Up through the field, emerging onto a good fast track. After approximately 1km, pass a track descending to the **R**, in a further 200m you come to a crossroads, **ignore** the tracks off to the left and right, but go through the gate **SA** and up the dirt singletrack into the woods. Superb, hard but rideable, climbing through the trees, emerges onto a level piece of track, but after a few short metres, breath recovered, branches off again **R** uphill. The track levels off onto boggy fast woodland singletrack; the twisty trail eventually ends at a gate.

➍ Through the double gates and downhill, fast and furious, to the woods and another gate, go **R** down the trail (**not SA**) and take the **L** fork where the bridleway splits. Follow the track up across the field and into the woods. **SA** through the woods. Where the track emerges, go **SA** down the parkland, (watch those jumps!) aiming for a small clump of trees. Finger posts mark the way. Turn **R** just before the trees and keep going across the Devonshires' front lawn towards the road.

➎ **L** down the road, soon branching off to the **L** onto a signed bridleway, back onto the road, then **L** signed *Edensor Tea Rooms*. **SA** keeping the church to your **L**. Up the road, then track, a good honest climb, go **SA** on the road at the top. Just beyond the brow of the hill, immediately after a farm track on the **L**, and before Ballcross Farm on the **R**, take the bridleway steeply down into the trees.

➏ Superb classic MTB descending brings one to the golf course, cross this (**danger** – imagine the embarrassment of being hit). Rejoin the road, and cruise back downhill, to the car park.

⟵🔗 **Making a day of it**

Choices, choices, choices. Turn onto the **Rowsley** loop (see page 137) (**GR SK 230670**) and follow it until the two rejoin in Lees Moor Wood (**GR SK 245670**) for a mammoth ride. Alternately, head up the road from Edensor to Pilsley (**GR SK 241710**) to run round the **Calver Circuit** (see page 55).

BELOW BASLOW EDGE

Calver Circuit – Central Peak

20km

Introduction

Just for a change we've started at the top of a hill. It's a short enough ride to prevent the last climb at the end from being too painful. The terrain is a real contrast between the fast, loose quarry tracks, some fantastic narrow limestone lanes and paths, and a loop of technical delight around the gritstone of Baslow Edge.

The Ride

Starting off with a wonderful fast chug over crag and moor, the route soon doubles back under Baslow Edge taking in superb technical singletrack before a road descent to Curbar then Calver villages. A grind up to Longstone Edge precedes a great mix of terrain as one traverses between the picturesque villages of Rowland, Hassop, Pilsley and Baslow. The final big long climb back up to Baslow Edge is a Peak classic. The last couple of kilometres are a good warm-down.

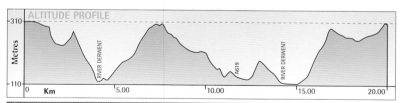

CALVER CIRCUIT　　　　　　　　　　　　　　　　　　　　**GRADE:** ▲

DISTANCE: 20KM

START/FINISH: CURBAR GAP

PARKING: PAY AND DISPLAY

PUBLIC HOUSE: THE MOON, STONEY MIDDLETON Tel: 01433 630 203

TOTAL ASCENT: 620M

GRID REFERENCE: SK 262747

CAFÉ: OUTSIDE, CALVER CROSSROADS Tel: 01433 631 111

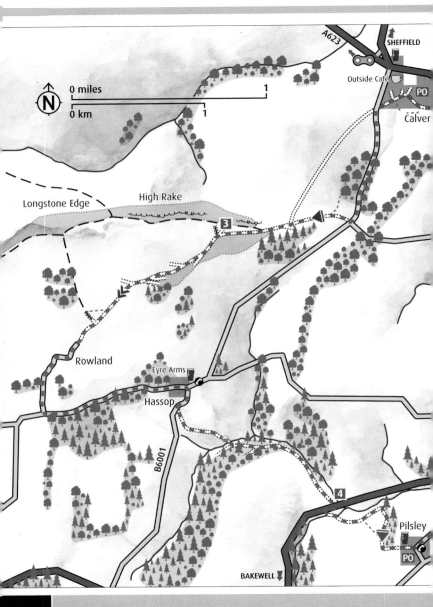

N

0 miles 1
0 km 1

A623

SHEFFIELD

Outside Café

Calver

PO

Longstone Edge

High Rake

3

Rowland

Eyre Arms

Hassop

B6001

4

Pilsley

PO

BAKEWELL

Calver Circuit

Directions – Calver Circuit

↦ Turn **R** out of the car park, **ignore** the first track on the **L**, but take the **second**, just beyond the brow of the hill. Through the gate, keep to the **L** on the main track, and race along the moor top. Turn **R** at the end, just past the Eagle Stone, passing the first small quarry and take the **R** fork underneath the next quarry (before the gate and descent proper). Follow this track down and then along under the edge. Variously technical. Continue more or less **SA** to meet the road.

2 **SA** down through the village. **R** at the bottom, then **R** onto the main road. Along the road for a short distance, then turn **L** into Calver Village. Follow the road, past the post office, then climb steeply to the main Bakewell road. Turn **L** and follow this road for 1km. At a crossroads, turn **R** uphill on the loose gravel track. Climb steeply up and up. **Ignore** the first track off to the left. Take the **second** track off to the **L** after 1km, keeping the large quarry to your left.

3 Descend the track, eventually joining tarmac and the village of Rowland. Pass through the village, turn **L** at the T-junction and drop down to Hassop, turning at the junction. Almost immediately turn **L** up the gravel farm track, past the hens, through the gates, then down the rocky roller coaster to the ford (wimps (me) and non-swimmers (my bike) can take the bridge). Up through the woods, along the track, to the road.

4 **R**, and take the first **L**, up the gravel track, and then more steep rutted climbing which soon levels out to emerge into Pilsley. **SA** down the road and **L** at the T-junction, to a large roundabout. Take the first exit into Baslow, **R** at the next roundabout, and then **SA** up into the village.

5 Pass the church and the Spar shop on the **L**, then go **SA** up Bar Road, and keep those pedals spinning all the way up. **L** at the T-junction half way up, to the fresh air once again of Baslow Edge. Keep **SA** past Wellington Monument, and a fast-paced romp over the moor to meet the road. **L** along the road, which leads back to the start after a couple of kilometres.

↤⊙⊙ Making a day of it

Turn off the ride at Calver (**GR SK 239748**) and run the **Great Longstone** route backwards (see page 73) to rejoin the **Calver Circuit** near Rowland (**GR SK 213721**).

Cheedale Wye Valley – Central Peak 23km

Introduction

Upon researching this ride, checking the maps, and knowing the terrain, I thought we were basically in for another one of those 'tracks 'n' roads' type rides: all very energetic, great views, but lacking in any real challenging true mountain bike riding. How wrong I was. This ride is surprisingly good. It packs in a huge amount of quality singletrack, great ups and superb downs. The terrain is some of the best the Peak can offer, and despite chunks of it being on the Pennine Bridleway, it is essential, unspoilt hardcore riding.

The Ride

The River Wye cuts a deep trench through the limestone of the Peak, with remarkable bridleways traversing and transecting it at several points – as does a disused railway line!

Starting pleasantly enough with a blast down the lane to Litton Mill, mountain biking proper kicks in with a stiff climb out of, and a descent back into, Cheedale. Some challenging singletrack leads onto the Monsal Head Viaduct, from where a state-of-the-art hill climb will test the best. The reward is some fantastic views and a pleasant traverse around to the Pennine Bridleway. The drop down into and climb out of Cheedale is mega, while some fantastic double – and singletrack takes you back round to Miller's Dale.

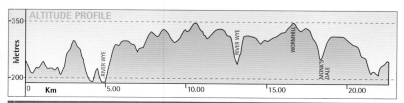

CHEEDALE WYE VALLEY GRADE: ▲

DISTANCE: 23KM
START/FINISH: MILLER'S DALE STATION
PARKING: MILLER'S DALE PAY AND DISPLAY
PUBLIC HOUSE: THE RED LION, LITTON Tel: 01298 871 458 or THREE SHIRES HEAD, WARDLOW MIRES Tel: 01298 872 268
TOTAL ASCENT: 879M
GRID REFERENCE: SK 138733
CAFÉ: OCCASIONAL TEA WAGON AT THE START

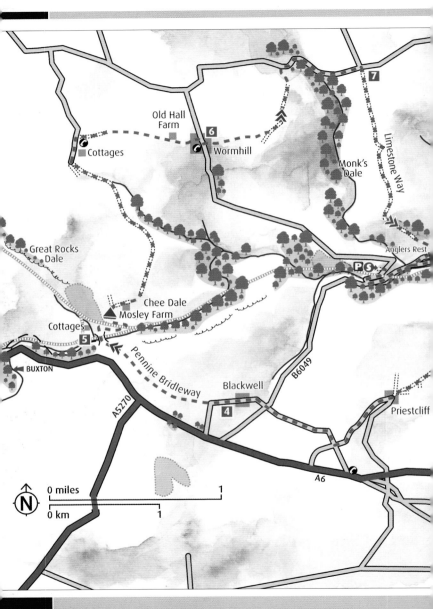

Cheedale Wye Valley

Directions – Cheedale Wye Valley

❺ Head out of the car park and **R** down the road to the junction, turning **L** and down the main road. Fork **R** onto the quiet lane towards Litton Mill, passing the Anglers Rest on the left. At the houses take the **L** fork uphill, **ignoring** the road down to Litton Mill. Uphill on tarmac then **SA** through a gate, signed footpath, up the track, zig-zag up the hill, take the track branching **R**, again signed as a footpath. Follow this to emerge on the road above Cressbrook. Turn **R** and descend **SA** to Cressbrook village.

2 Upon entering the village, take the **R** fork downhill, and keep heading downhill, **SA** on the road, along the valley floor. Follow this road for a couple of kilometres, taking a track to the **R** just as the road starts to climb. Follow the bridleway sign to excellent steady singletrack climbing uphill, turning downhill as the trail runs up to the road; descend fast, towards the viaduct. Cross this, and head along the track for 200m, taking the track off to the **L**, after the 'station' signed *Brushfield*. Climb up to the junction, **R** uphill onto polished raw limestone. This is one of the classic hill climbs of the Peak. Good Luck.

3 The lane eventually flattens out, with fantastic views once you've wiped the blood and sweat from your eyes. Keep **SA** to descend into the hamlet of Brushfield. Keep **SA** up the lane, signed *Priestcliffe*. Keep **SA** on this lane, turning sharp **L**, then downhill, sweeping **L** at the junction with the old-looking New Barn on the right. **SA** to the small village of Priestcliffe. Take the **R** fork in the road, and turn **R** at the next crossroads. Keep **SA** on tarmac, **SA** at the next crossroads, and through the small village of Blackwell.

4 The tarmac starts to deteriorate, **SA** onto the Pennine Bridleway, where the road swings left. Follow the *Pennine Bridleway* signs, through the distinctive horse friendly gates and keep **L** at the first junction of tracks, i.e. **ignore** the track heading off straight downhill. As the track swings back towards the road, keep **L** and follow those gates and Pennine Bridleway, downhill, excellent, over the disused railway, and down **SA** towards the river. Cross this.

5 Turn **R** and follow the excellent grassy track steadily uphill (and up and up) emerging into Mosley Farm. **SA** through the farm, taking the road back out. **SA** up the lane to join the road, then just after a row of cottages and a telephone box on the **R**, turn **R** onto a track, towards Wormhill, keep **SA** on this track, which briefly disappears, and **SA** up the hill, keep wall on your right. Drop through the farm-yard, turn **R** onto the road.

6 Almost immediately **L** onto the signed public bridleway. Brilliant riding, watch out for the sharp turn **L**, down onto walled singletrack, emerging into the valley bottom of Monk's Dale, bear **L** to the gap in the wall and the road. Turn **R** uphill on tarmac, turning **R** down a track at the crossroads after the farmhouse, just under 1km from Monk's Dale.

7 Rutty singletrack and doubletrack fun descends with speed and abandon down to the farm – keep up the pace to outrun the dog. Keep **SA** downhill onto a loose and rocky bit of lane. Turn **R** onto the small road, and **SA** onto the main road. **SA** under the viaduct, past the craft shop, then **R** back uphill turning **L** into the car park. Good wasn't it?

◄⊙⊙ Making a day of it

When you reach the bottom of the valley at Monsal Head, (**GR SK 178718**), you'll be excited to know that you're at the start of the course used in the annual **Monsal Head Hill Climb**. Hammer up the road as fast as is physically possible and try not to vomit at the top. Anything under two minutes is a good effort, a one-thirty would probably put you a nice way up the rankings.

ABOVE LITTON MILL

BONSALL WOODS

Cromford Circuit – South Peak

21.3km

Introduction

What makes a bad ride? Grassy fields, busy roads, carries, overgrown trails, convoluted routes. It is often a fine line between good and bad, not withstanding the day to day variables of weather, rider and the like. Some rides can have a heap of the above features, yet still be good, while some can have only a few bad points, but be poor. Of course this is dependant on whether you've got up off the sofa in the first place. I tend to choose a ride either because a) it's my local favourite circuit, b) it's a classic round, c) it's got great technical bits to fit my mood, or d) and here's the point I'm getting to, it traverses a part of the country I've never seen – it's a tour.

Cromford is a great tour traversing a part of the world few mountain bikers get to. It is a good lap of the area, has some historic interest and the car parking only costs 50p!

The Ride

Set off from Black Rocks car park, and warm up (and up and up) westbound along the High Peak Trail. Turn north to Grangemill along fast, satisfying tracks and paths. Roads, tracks and challenging singletrack bring you to a great descent into the village of Bonsall, where a choice of routes lead into Cromford. An excellent fast climb out, followed by a dull grassy field section leads to more good tracks and a descent back to the start.

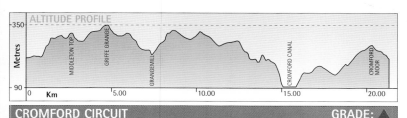

CROMFORD CIRCUIT | GRADE: ▲

DISTANCE: 21.3KM
START/FINISH: CROMFORD
PARKING: BLACK ROCKS
PUBLIC HOUSE: THE RISING SUN, MIDDLETON Tel: 01629 822 420

TOTAL ASCENT: 675M
GRID REFERENCE: SK 290555
CAFÉ: SCARTHIN BOOKS CAFÉ, CROMFORD Tel: 01629 823 272

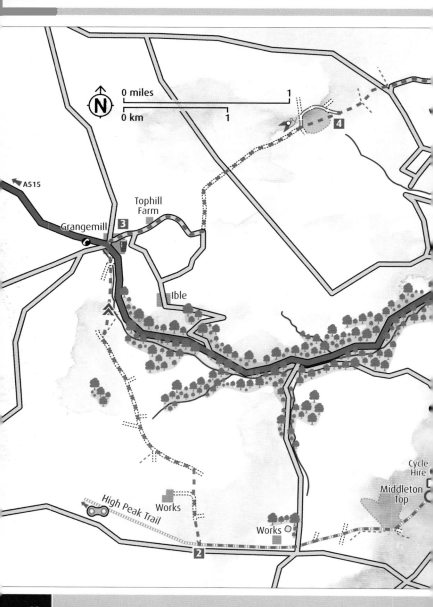

Cromford Circuit

Directions – Cromford Circuit

➊ From the car park set off on the level cinder High Peak Trail, heading west. Cross the bridge over the road, past the light railway and over two more roads to a long steady climb up to a view point and a flat fast trail to another climb. The trail levels off, and runs parallel to a road on the left. After a factory and a small building on the left, a signed bridleway heads off across fields to the **R**.

2 Take this (if you reach a gate where the trail diverges from the road you've gone too far). Head across the field, over some stiles by gates and the trail soon becomes a track, which turns left into some large buildings. Go **SA** where the track swings left, down a fine fast bridleway to join a larger track. Follow this turning **L**, then downhill, ignoring a leftwards branch up to a farm. Down then back up, through some gates, looking out for a turn **R** signed bridleway to *Grangemill*. Take this good singletrack down through the cow field to the crossroads, pub and hubbub of Grangemill.

3 Go **SA** up the road, immediately turning **R** up the lane to Ible, go **SA** up this road, ignoring the right turn to Ible and climb steeply past the scruffy farm to a crossroads of lanes and tracks. As the road turns sharp right, turn sharp **L** on the track and descend to the road, go **SA** across the road onto another broad track towards a large hole in the ground. Either go **SA** and descend into the hole and slog out the other side (along with all the other scrambling types), the fun option, **OR** turn **L**, uphill for a short way, taking the track on the **R** around the hole, then **SA** downhill, passing the gate on the left and the gate on the right leading into the quarry. Then **SA** down the path; the conservative (and better) option.

4 Descend Moorland Lane, a narrow walled singletrack, keeping to the main path, swinging **L** then **SA** down to the road. **SA** over the road, and then **SA** up the next road looking out for a track (no sign) on the **R** just after a signed footpath (and also 150m before a signed bridleway leads off left). Follow this track, (excellent descent), looking out for a **L** turn just before some rock steps, and the start of the tunnel of trees. Take this **L** turn (actually best to take the second **L**, just after the first, and just after the little rock steps). Follow the narrow bridleway past a stile on the right.

5 The bridleway eventually swings **R**, turning downhill onto concrete to emerge at the quaint village cross in Bonsall. Descend on the main road **SA** to a junction, turn **L** to Cromford. **OR** from the village cross Church Lane leads off **L**, you can follow this, which soon becomes a bridletrack, alongside a quarry for a couple of kilometres. The track splits (the abrupt end of the bridleway), and a footpath goes **R** downhill to a zig-zag and descent to the main road, if you do take this option make sure you observe the right of way of walkers and **push/carry your bike down this short link-up**.

6 Head into the busy world of Cromford, turn **L** down to the lights, turning **R**, then down the A6, looking out for the small lane off to the **R**, Intake Lane. Take this, uphill, eventually becoming a pleasant woodland climb. Under the bridge, the track turns **R**, then back **L** to descend past the caravan site to the road. Turn **R**, up the road, looking out for a track down to Meerbrook Farm. Take this, turning off **L** just before the farm, through the gates for a trudge up through the fields, before a good track descends down to a road. Turn **R** and descend into the village, going **SA** where the road turns **L**, under the bridge and **R** into the car park.

◄◉ Making a day of it

The **Cromford Circuit** runs briefly along the High Peak Trail. Follow this past the point where the route turns off (**GR SK 256546**) and you're on the **Grangemill** circuit (see page 19). Keep going and you'll hit the **Middleton** ride near Gotham (**GR SK 198586**) (see page 31). Follow this circuit round, meet the Grangemill at roughly the same spot, follow that in reverse to Grangemill itself (**GR SK 243576**) and finish the original ride.

FRED YONG AND TOM FENTON

DESCENDING INTO ROWLAND

Great Longstone – Central Peak   19.5/11km

Introduction

This short ride gives a great flavour of the White Peak, and can even be attempted in the wet winter months. Great views, some lovely trails and rocky descents all combine to leave the rider wanting more.

The Ride

Limited parking is available in the village of Great Longstone, with alternative parking readily available at Monsal Head, a short ride from the start. The ride begins with quite a climb, up, up and up (mud, mud and mud in the winter) to reach the road before heading around Longstone Moor, and down the usually puddly quarry tracks to Black Harry Gate. A pleasant climb takes you back up to the edge, and a full-on rocky descent drops back down into the village of Rowland and a short ride to Great Longstone. The long version climbs steeply in the opposite direction from Black Harry Gate. It barrels down to the main road and climbs through the village of Eyam, before a swift descent leads back to Stoney Middleton. A short road section leads you to the bottom of a long climb back up to Longstone Edge and the final descent to Rowland.

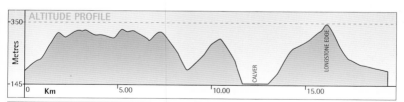

ALTITUDE PROFILE

Metres

CALVER

LONGSTONE EDGE

Km   5.00   10.00   15.00

GREAT LONGSTONE   GRADE: ▲

DISTANCE: 19.5KM (FULL) or 11KM (SHORT)
START/FINISH: GREAT LONGSTONE
PARKING: ON STREET
PUBLIC HOUSE: THREE STAGS HEAD, WARDLOW MIRES Tel: 1298 872 268

TOTAL ASCENT: 660M (FULL) or 352M (SHORT)
GRID REFERENCE: SK 200719
CAFÉ: OUTSIDE, CALVER CROSSROADS Tel: 01433 631 111

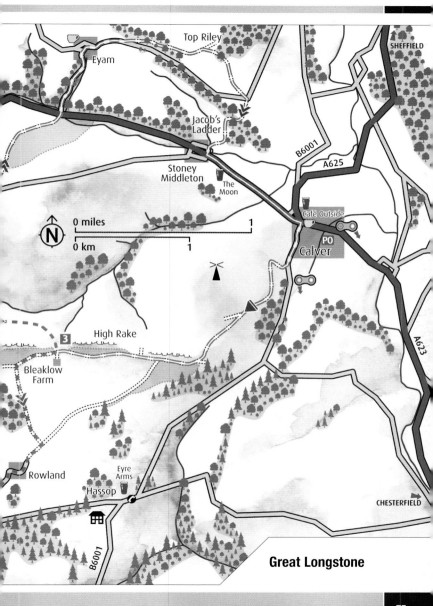

Top Riley

SHEFFIELD

Eyam

Jacob's
Ladder

B6001

A625

Stoney
Middleton

The Moon

Café Outside

PO

Calver

N

0 miles   1

0 km   1

A623

High Rake

3

Bleaklow
Farm

Rowland

Eyre
Arms

Hassop

CHESTERFIELD

B6001

Great Longstone

Directions – Great Longstone

➎ Head west out of the village, taking Moor Lane on the **R**, and then a **L** up the track to Dale Farm 200m up the lane. Follow the track, always rideable, but hard enough, up the hill, eventually levelling off to meet the road. Turn **R** and head up the hill, taking the first tarmac lane on the **R**. Follow this, again taking the first tarmac lane on the **R** after 1km.

2 After 200m, take the bridletrack off to the **L** descending to the large slurry pond. Traverse this on the track to a crossroads of usually muddy tracks in the dip. Turn **R** through the small gate, and then almost immediately **L**, on to a pleasant steady climb, up above Coombs Dale. Head between the quarry workings to meet a larger track.

3 Turn **R** up the track, past the farm set back on the **L**. Look out for a bridleway heading off to the **L**, before the next climb. This is level at first, but soon descends sharply, very rocky with drops, and can be lethal in the wet, but great fun in the dry. Drop down **SA** to meet a larger track, turn **R** and descend into Rowland. The lane meets the road, turn **R** and head back keeping **SA** to Great Longstone.

This ride can be extended to turn it into a fine afternoon excursion, with a café en route.

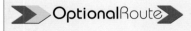

Option B:
From Black Harry Gate, turn **L** up the steep track and follow it **SA**, crossing a minor road down to the main road, watching out for quarry traffic. Go **SA** and follow the road up and round to the **R** through the village of Eyam. As the houses end, turn **L** up towards Top Riley and then **R** into the woods. Follow the track down **R**, through gates and fields to the road. **SA** onto the obvious and very fast track down into Stoney Middleton and follow your nose to the main road. Turn **L** along this to Calver crossroads, **R** up the hill and take the gated track on the **R** after 400m, just after the end of the houses. The track zig-zags up and eventually eases a little, where you take the **L** fork. Continue up, bearing **R** at the big junction of tracks, **ignoring** turnings off to the left. Keep **SA** on the main track with huge quarry workings to your right, which brings you back to (**3**).

◄⚙ **Making a day of it**

Three routes meet in Calver – the **Great Longstone** ride (see page 73), the **Quarry Trail** (see page 37) and the **Calver Circuit** (see page 55). Ride one, ride two – try and do all three in a day for a big-mile challenge.

Introduction

A gruelling, unforgiving ride, short in distance, high in ascent. Essentially three challenging climbs – with equally exciting descents. This is pure mountain biking, at times remote, at times exhausting and taking in some of the best landscape and views the Peak District can offer. If your American mate was coming over from Moab – this is where you should take them (leave them).

The Ride

Leaving Hayfield, climb up the Snake Path, onto Middle Moor, under the shadow of Kinder Scout, before dropping down and climbing up over Lantern Pike, a distinctly friendly climb. Then drop rapidly down to cross the River Sett, before a long climb on road and track leads to that ever so superb ascent of Chinley Churn. Not particularly technical, but a great one to crack. Over the Churn and you drop down to Stubbs Farm, and a painful traverse of a rough meadow, before a fantastic technical singletrack plunge back into Hayfield.

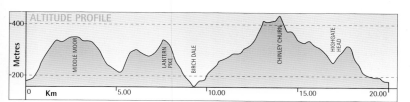

HAYFIELD — **GRADE:** ▲

DISTANCE: 20KM
START/FINISH: HAYFIELD PAY AND DISPLAY
PARKING: HAYFIELD PAY AND DISPLAY, ON THE SETT VALLEY TRAIL
PUBLIC HOUSE: THE WALTZING WEASEL Tel: 01663 743 402

TOTAL ASCENT: 779M
GRID REFERENCE: SK 035870
CAFÉ: GRUMBLEYS Tel: 01663 741 444

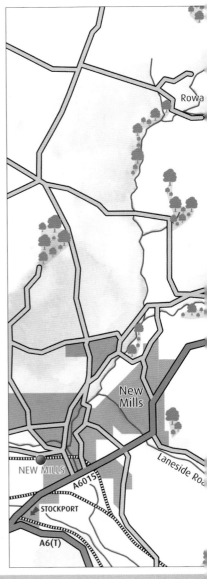

Rowa

New
Mills

NEW MILLS

Laneside Roa

A6015

STOCKPORT

A6(T)

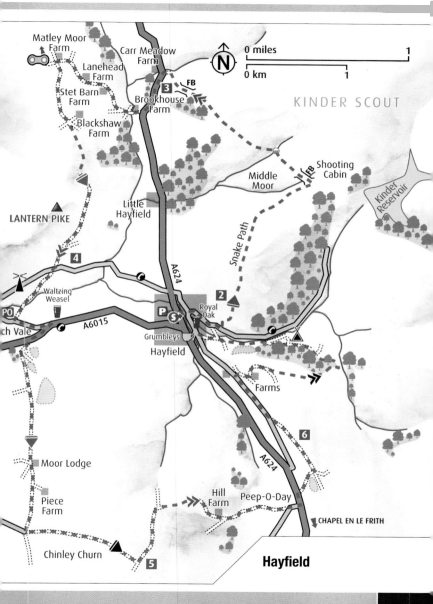

Matley Moor Farm

Carr Meadow Farm

Lanehead Farm

3 FB

Stet Barn Farm

Brookhouse Farm

KINDER SCOUT

Blackshaw Farm

FB Shooting Cabin

Middle Moor

Kinder Reservoir

Little Hayfield

LANTERN PIKE

Snake Path

4

Waltzing Weasel

2

PO

A624

Royal Oak

A6015

Grumbleys

Hayfield

ch Vale

Farms

6

Moor Lodge

A624

Piece Farm

Hill Farm

Peep-O-Day

CHAPEL EN LE FRITH

Chinley Churn

5

Hayfield

Directions – Hayfield

➎ Leave the car park heading east and use the pedestrian and bridleway crossing over the busy road to enter Hayfield. **L** on the road, then fork **R** uphill towards Kinder Reservoir, and **SA** up the road. Look out for the track (Snake Path) on the **L**, take this up cobbles and through a gate onto a steeper, challenging section, which soon eases, becoming a pleasant, but long climb up through gates onto the moors.

2 **SA** vaguely heading for a distinctive white cabin. Just before this turn **L** across a long footbridge and follow the track over Middle Moor, crossing one stream, before a very fast descent to another stream and the road.

3 Turn **L** downhill, and take the first road on the **R**, **SA** up the lane past Stet Barn Farm and Lane Head Farm, all uphill, before the road levels out. Swing **L** at Matley Moor Farm, down the track. At the end of the track, go **SA** into the field, following the bridleway sign, and cross the field, aiming for a gate in the far **L** corner. Through the gate, and follow the good track uphill, then downhill, becoming tarmac, to suddenly emerge onto a road.

4 More or less **SA** over the road, taking the lane and bridleway cutting back downhill. More exciting descent, soon emerging onto another road. Turn **L**, and climb up to the main road. Turn **R** along this for 200m, forking **L** uphill on Quarry Lane. Steady climbing emerges onto the moor, go past Moor Lodge, where the tarmac gives way to track. Turn **L** onto a bridleway, at the crossroads, where Lanehead Road (tarmac) comes up from the right. The climb is roughly split into three, the first section is a straightforward bit of walled track, refreshingly shared with a happy little stream. The second is an easy cruise up to a gate. The third is a superb, lung bursting, grind. Nowhere overly technical, just focus on the fingerpost at the top, and keep it going.

5 At the top turn **L** along the rutted track, to a gate. Turn **R**, not straight ahead, across the rough moor, undulating along, keeping the wall and fence to your right. The track soon becomes walled, before a good descent to Hill Farm. **Please walk through the garden**, sticking to the bridleway. Follow the good track steeply down to join the main road. Turn **L** and head downhill, taking the bridleway on the **R**, just before a small farmhouse. Follow this to a crossroads of tracks, turn **L** downhill and **SA** to join a small tarmac lane.

6 Fast downhill, looking out of a track and bridleway off to the **R**, just after the first buildings on the right, and opposite the first buildings on the left. Follow the track, to a gate and field. Into the field, and **SA**, following a few posts heading to the right-hand edge of the trees. At the trees, go through the gate and downhill, quite technical with a few tricky bits. All superb stuff, turn **L** at the bridleway T-junction, and more superb singletrack descend to the valley bottom, and a blast back into Hayfield. Retrace your steps to the car.

◄◯◯ Making a day of it

When you reach Matley Moor Farm (**GR SK 024896**), you've met the **Rowarth Circuit** on page 28 of our best-selling **Dark Peak Mountain Biking – True Grit Trails** guide. In true entrepreneurial style, we're not going give you directions, but we will tell you that you can run it in reverse from this point and pick up the **Hayfield** ride once more near Wethercotes (**GR SK 023875**).

MIDDLE MOOR

JON BARTON CLIMBING UP TO HOLY MOOR

Holymoorside – East Peak

Introduction

A fantastic technical mountain bike ride with good stretches of challenging singletrack, linked by pleasant stretches of track and lane. Like much of the riding in the area it is best attempted in the summer, although in moderate conditions only the climb up from Birley Brook is a muddy problem.

The Ride

Starting from Linacre Reservoirs the ride warms up easily enough along a pleasant trail, before dropping down to Birley Brook, with interest, to a twisty climb back out that is fantastic – when it's dry. The route then climbs up onto the moors, for some quintessential singletrack action, and a steep descent down Hungerhill Lane. More great climbing and fast descending undulates the route north, before a final descent to the reservoir all too quickly brings the ride to an end.

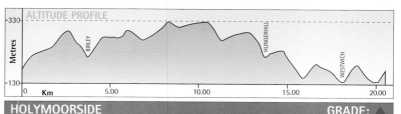

HOLYMOORSIDE GRADE: ▲

DISTANCE: 21KM
START/FINISH: LINACRE RESERVOIRS
PARKING: FREE PARKING AT RESERVOIRS
PUBLIC HOUSE: THE GATE INN, OVERGREEN Tel: 01246 276 923
TOTAL ASCENT: 570M
GRID REFERENCE: SK 334729
CAFÉ: ICE CREAM VAN IN CAR PARK IF WEATHER IS GOOD

Holymoorside

Directions – Holymoorside

➤ From the first parking bay on the right, head **R** downhill for a few metres, taking the bridleway on the **R**, which runs alongside the woods. Through a gate and **SA** across a field to another gate and a lane which leads to the road. Turn **L** and follow the road for approximately 1km, turning **L** down Birley Lane. Follow the tarmac lane downhill, going **SA** where it swings to the left to a house.

2 Follow the grassy bridleway through the woods to emerge on a tarmac track, opposite a pond. Turn **L** along the track, through the impressive gates down to *Birley Farm*, cross the cattle-grid and go **SA** across the mown strip to pick up the descending bridleway down to Birley Brook. Cross this, usually boggy for 50m or so, then climb with interest (or cursing guidebook writers if wet) to emerge in Wigley.

3 At the road go **SA** through the village of Wadshelf and turn **R** on the main road. After approximately 1km turn **L**, just after the large pub, down Game Lea Lane, down this track, past two farms, past the pigs, get chased by the dog, turning **L** where the track splits, (**SA** goes up to a third farm).

4 At the road turn **R** and go **SA** at the T-junction onto open moorland and a vague bridleway. Follow this, descending with skill, to the road. Turn **R** and follow the road for 300m, past a farm on the right, and take the bridleway to the **L** at the next farm on the **L**. Follow the bridleway signs to superb singletrack across the moor. **SA** through double gates, and **SA** at the next set of double gates, **SA** at a junction of tracks, (farm house on the left). Carry on to meet Walton Lees Farm. Turn **L** at the farm.

5 Descend the track, keeping **SA** at the junction. Descend steeply down Hungerhill Lane, now sadly surfaced, cross the bridge and climb up to the road. Turn **R** on the road, looking out for a bridleway heading off uphill to the **L** after a good couple of hundred metres. Good technical climbing soon leads to quality singletrack, keep **SA**, eventually dropping down to the road. **R**, downhill, take the first road on the **L**, at the edge of the village.

6 Follow the road, **R** at the junction, then **R** and immediately **L** at the busy main road, taking the lane just after the garage forecourt. **SA**, to a more broken lane, follow this **SA**, turning **L**, on the bridleway down to the river, just before Broomhall Farm. The track leads down to and across a stream with a pleasant climb up to the road. Turn **L** and head up the road, past the church, taking the next **R**, a good descent down into the woods, keep **SA** to meet the lane, turn **L** and climb back up to the car park.

🔗 Making a day of it

The **Holymoorside** route could have been called 'Linacre South' as it shares its start/finish car park with the **Linacre North** ride (see page 25). Instead of riding the final kilometre or so of the loop, drop down Grange Hill (**GR SK 316736**) to Grange Lumb Farm and the **Linacre North** route.

BERESFORD 'SHORE'

Manifold Valley – South Peak   24.5km

Introduction

If you want to tick every corner of the White Peak and you enjoy a good high-speed romp across some stunning Peak District landscape then this is essential riding. If you are new to mountain biking, or indeed have the family along for the day, then you've come to the right place. If you want hardcore trails and demanding terrain, turn the page. The ride is more or less split into thirds, good quality singletrack, quiet easy going tracks and lanes, and paved cycleway. On a quiet evening I often pick this route for its solitude and peaceful snap-shot of the flora, fauna and environment of the Peak.

The Ride

Starting from beside the village duck pond in Hartington, this ride heads up over a spur of Wolfcote Hill and then back down the dry valley of Biggin Dale, with a short push back out the other side. This is followed by a challenging drop into Beresford Dale and then a climb up around Narrowdale Hill before grand views and speedy descending takes you into the Manifold Valley among a peloton of family cyclists, up to Hulme End. Quiet lanes and a bit of retracing your steps takes you back to Hartington.

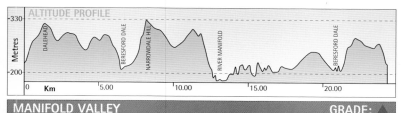

ALTITUDE PROFILE

DALEHEAD · BERESFORD DALE · NARROWDALE HILL · RIVER MANIFOLD · BERESFORD DALE

Metres — 330, 200

Km 0 · 5.00 · 10.00 · 15.00 · 20.00

MANIFOLD VALLEY   GRADE: ▲

DISTANCE: 24.5KM

START/FINISH: HARTINGTON

PARKING: ON STREET IN VILLAGE CENTRE

PUBLIC HOUSE: THE DEVONSHIRE ARMS, HARTINGTON Tel: 01298 84 232

TOTAL ASCENT: 770M

GRID REFERENCE: SK 128604

CAFÉ: BERESFORD TEA ROOMS, HARTINGTON Tel: 01298 844 188

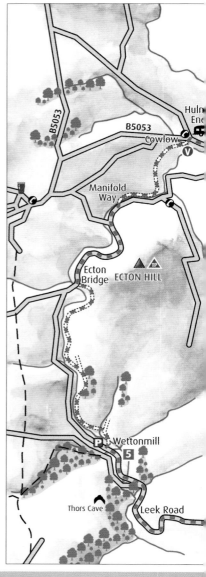

Manifold Valley

Directions – Manifold

➊ Starting from the centre of Hartington leave the village east on the B5054, taking the first **R** uphill on High Cross Lane, signed to the *Youth Hostel*. Go past the hostel and take the lane on the **R** after approximately 150m. Follow this well surfaced lane **SA** up, then down to join the road. Keep **SA**, taking the first **R** uphill, and then steadily down looking out for a signed bridleway on the **R**; take this.

➋ A good fun descent leads down into the dale, turn **R** at the bottom, heading up the dale, then following the bridleway up the steep hill, onto a better track and then a lane. Keep **SA** for 500m, and then take the bridleway **L**, down the rocky trail to the road, turn **R**, and then first **R** down into Beresford Dale.

➌ Go **SA** across the bridge. Turn **R** and follow the singletrack to a gate and keep **SA** up the dale. Turn **R** at the junction and follow the track up to the farm, nestled at the base of the conical Narrowdale Hill. At the farm turn **L**, up the track between the buildings then **SA** through the gates and steeply up the hill. Where the trail levels off, and before the first stone stile, turn **R** up to the hill, then follow the bridleway back **L** and then down the good track, past the camping barn to a T-junction of tracks. Turn **R** to the road.

➍ **R** along the lane for 400m, then **L** down the lane, **L** at the T-junction and **SA** into the village of Wetton. Turn **R** at the T-junction in the village, then take the first **L**, keep **R** at the next junction, descending the steep road towards the Manifold Valley, with good views of Thor's Cave on the opposite side of the dale.

➎ Follow the dale upstream to Wetton Mill, turn **R** to the mill, then take the track **L** heading upstream for a couple of gentle kilometres before once again joining the road and heading **R** and then, after about 1km, down **L** across the river and onto the family cycleway upstream to Hulme End. Turn **R** on the road then take the first **R** after 500m. Heading **SA** at the crossroads, on Beresford Lane down to Beresford Dale. Just before the bridge over the river, turn **R** along the vague lane across the field. This joins the route out at a gateway – usually with barbed wire instead of a gate.

➏ Cross the stile on the right of the gateway, and head acutely back **L** along the narrow trail back down to the bridge across the River Dove. A good little jump off the end of the bridge, then **SA** uphill, taking the **R** turn on the more amenable track up to the road. Turn **L** and follow the lane for 600m taking the track **SA** where the lane swings **R**. Follow the lane to the road, turn **L** downhill, and **L** again back into Hartington.

 Making a day of it

Take the family and pick up the nearby Pennine Bridleway (where it runs along the Tissington Trail). See the 'Family Rides' section on page 156 for more details.

South Buxton Circuit – West Peak

25km

Introduction

Another corner of the Peak that rarely sees the mountain bike masses, but riddled with great trails all the same. Take some time to explore this area and you will be rewarded with good days out around seldom visited little hamlets and quiet byways. Tell someone where you are going and don't speak to the locals!

As part of our ride we have included a couple of extreme descents – by far the toughest in the area – while great challenges, they are quite short and are easily walked down by the sane.

The Ride

Starting with a great view and a blast across the broad valley bottom of the River Dove, the ride then climbs up to the great ridge of limestone south of Buxton, which it traverses west before heading south, past the source of the River Dove. It then drops back down, via a series of extreme rocky steps, to cross the river at Tenterhill, before a push back out and another crossing at Hollinsclough. Yet more extremely technical downhill terrain leads to a pleasant run back to Longnor.

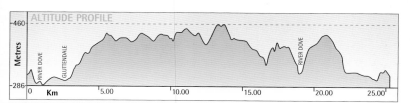

ALTITUDE PROFILE

SOUTH BUXTON CIRCUIT

GRADE: ▲

DISTANCE: 25KM
START/FINISH: LONGNOR
PARKING: LONGNOR CAR PARK
TOTAL ASCENT: 530M
GRID REFERENCE: SK 088649
CAFÉ: FIVEWAYS CAFÉ, JUNCTION OF DALE RD/LONDON RD/HIGH ST (BUXTON)
PUBLIC HOUSE: THE QUIET WOMAN, EARL STERNDALE Tel: 01298 83 211

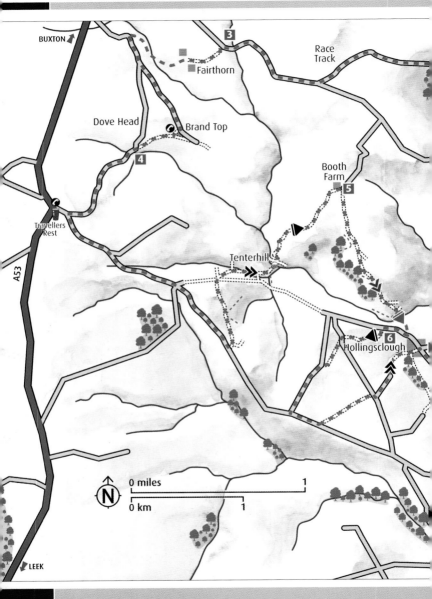

BUXTON

3

Race
Track

Fairthorn

Dove Head

Brand Top

4

Booth
Farm

5

Travellers
Rest

A53

Tenterhill

6

Hollingsclough

N

0 miles   1

0 km   1

LEEK

Directions – South Buxton Circuit

5 Exit the car park turning **R** and on the edge of town take the **L** turn up the tarmac lane signposted to *The Ridge*. Follow the track steeply down, then **SA** across the valley bottom, over the bridge and just before the track starts climbing, and 100m before the road, take the farm track and bridleway **L**. Go **SA** past the farm and a fast track, through gates, leads to the road at Glutton Bridge. Turn **R** and climb steeply up Glutton Dale keeping **SA** until after approximately 3km, upon the brow of the hill, a signed bridleway leads off **L**.

2 Steadily uphill on variously well-defined grassy tracks. Through a gate, bearing **L**, then downhill through another gate following the track down to a gate and the road. **Don't** go onto the road, take the gate to the **R** and follow the bridleway running parallel to the road. Avoid falling into the quarry on the **R**. Join the road at the next gate. Turn **R** and head uphill, round the bend, past the racetrack up round another hill, and look out for a signed bridleway down a track to the **L**.

3 Descend the track to Fairthorn Farm, turn **R** in front of the house, over the mown strip, picking up a more defined bridleway which climbs up the valley, with a few tricky bits, before turning **L** to cross the stream and climb up to the road. Turn **L** onto the road and take the **L** fork as the road splits, descending to a house on the **R**. Take the track on the **R**, immediately after the house, and descend this to the road.

4 Turn **L** and climb steeply up tarmac to a T-junction (**don't** turn right to the Travellers Rest!). **L** downhill passing a lane off to the left, then **SA** at a crossroads, looking out for a signed bridleway to the **L**. Descend this increasingly exciting rutted singletrack, to the farm, exit onto the road, then take the track **SA**, bearing off to the **R**, past the buildings. Take a deep breath, remove that part of your brain which controls logic, tighten the helmet, and award yourself a medal if you reach the stream in one piece. Tenterhill is one of the hardest rocky descents in the Peak, extreme for the last 200m down to the stream. Enjoy. Cross the stream and unfortunately push your bike back up the other side. Ride along the more amenable track to Booth Farm.

5 Turn **R** out of the farm, not up the road but **R** down the bridleway, excellent, steady pleasant descending, ignoring all **L** turns, until a sign **R** zigzags indistinctly down to a ford, cross this, pass the footbridge on the **L**, then head off uphill to the **R**, climbing up to meet the road.

6   Turn **R** uphill, taking a **L** up a very steep track to join a road, cross this **SA** and follow the good track, soon reaching another road, turn **L** and climb up to a T-junction. Turn **L** and look out for a good track off to the **L** after 150m. Whatever is left of your bike and skeleton after Tenterhill will not escape trauma on this bad boy of a lane that thinks it's a rockface. A lady with a crown awaits the successful at the bottom for their well-deserved knighthood. Exit onto the road.

7   Turn **R** and follow the pleasant road **SA**, to a T-junction, **L** up the steep hill back into Longnor.

◄☉☉ Making a day of it

When you reach Tenterhill (**GR SK 051673**), stop, lower your saddle and turn to page 162 for a play on the various descents in the area. All good fun, especially if you try and ride back up them again...

DON'T TALK TO THE LOCALS

SECTION 3

Enduros

Now we're talking. Pack your sarnies and your chain lube. These are big, tough rides (for big, tough riders?) that'll probably take you all day. They're challenging routes for fit and experienced mountain bikers – you know, 'proper' rides. Rides you might describe as 'a bit of a beast'.

Enduros

sponsored by  **COTIC**

www.cotic.co.uk

DROPPING DOWN THE STANAGE PLANTATION PHOTO: JOHN COEFIELD

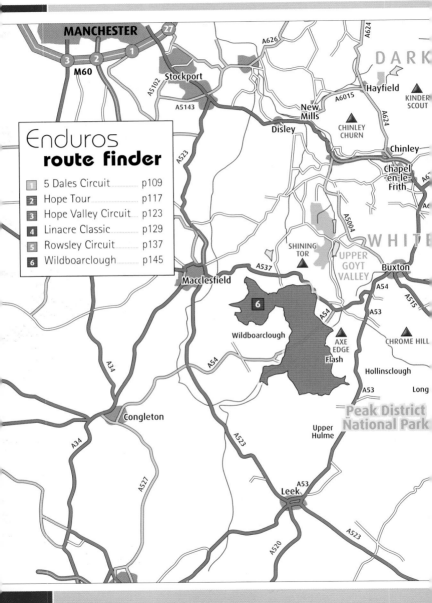

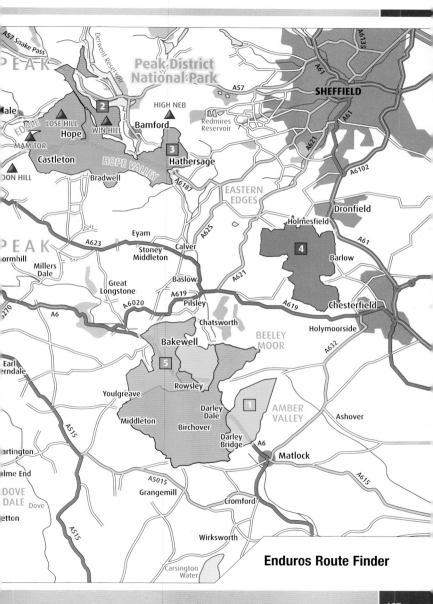

Enduros Route Finder

CLIMBING UP CALTON PASTURES PHOTO: JOHN COEFIELD

5 Dales Circuit – Central Peak

Introduction

This long, hard and varied route is best done in the summer, when the superb woodland singletrack can be enjoyed in all its swoopy finery. The views from Beeley Moor are superb, while the last hairpins on the climb of Rowsley Bar, scene of the National Hill Climb Championship (just over five minutes floor to summit – if you fancy a go) are a great aerobic burn out. However, this is just the beginning, the route keeps heading into and back out of dale after dale, sometimes on super-fast descents, sometimes on singletrack climbs, hard tarmac slogs or just good old honest farm tracks. A brilliant ride – one of the best in this book, taking in all that the heart of the White Peak has to offer.

The Ride

From Darley Bridge, climb out on the long hill east towards Beeley Moor, before a good descent and a big dollop of fine singletrack traverses around to climb back up towards Beeley Moor once again. The route then drops down to cross the River Derwent and climbs to Calton Pastures, before ascending on brilliant woodland trails and crossing the River Wye at Haddon Hall. Steady farm track work leads to yet another great woodland singletrack descent to cross Lathkill Dale, en route to the River Bradford, and so onwards to Birchover, crossing Ivy Bar Brook on the way. A super-fast descent of Oldfield Lane brings the weary rider back to the start.

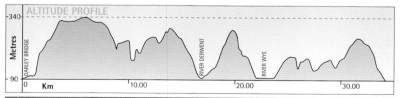

5 DALES CIRCUIT   GRADE: ▲

DISTANCE: 36KM

START/FINISH: DARLEY BRIDGE

PARKING: DARLEY BRIDGE FREE CAR PARK

PUBLIC HOUSE: THREE STAGS HEAD, DARLEY BRIDGE Tel: 01629 732 358

TOTAL ASCENT: 1,074M

GRID REFERENCE: SK 270620

CAFÉ: JUST OFF ROUTE, ELTON CAFÉ, ELTON Tel: 01629 650 217

CHESTERFIELD

CHATSWORTH

BUXTON

Bakewell

A619

B6048

A6

Haddon
Hall

4

B5056

Youlgreave

FB

FB

continues on
NEXT PAGE

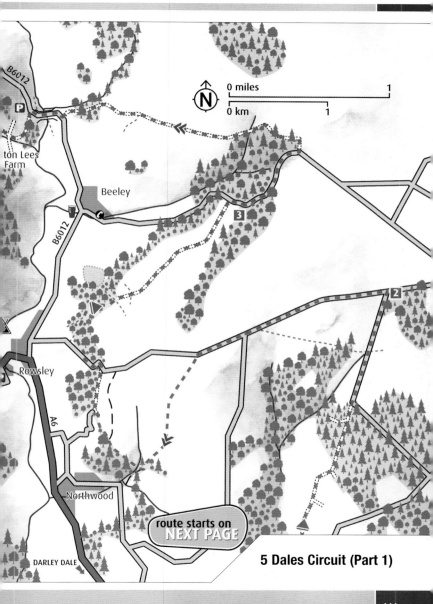

route starts on
NEXT PAGE

5 Dales Circuit (Part 1)

BAKEWELL

continued from
LAST PAGE

Haddon
Hall

A6

4

Nutseats
Quarry

B5056

FB

Youlgreave

FB

5

0 miles   1

N

0 km   1

B5056

Druids Inn

Birchover

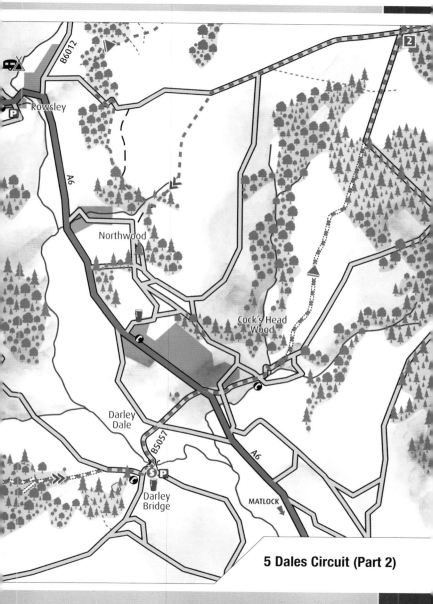

5 Dales Circuit (Part 2)

Directions – 5 Dales Circuit

5▸ L out of car park along B5057 for 800m, cross the A6 and then 800m on the same B road to the start of the climb. Steep hairpins lead to a row of terraced cottages, turn L after last house up the rough and tough track, joining Flash Lane to crossroads.

2 L onto road to the brow of Rowsley Bar climb, then L through double gates onto a bridleway. Descend on the obvious track, then keep R along the contouring woodland bridleway, passing through the two gates where the track intersects. At the road, descend via two hairpins and take farm track R just after house, climbing for 200m until bridleway drops L into woods, then climbs sharply to wooden bridge. Turn sharp R after bridge and climb via gates into fields, and take the farm track between buildings heading **NE** to join the main road

3 Turn R onto Beeley Hill for 1km, L at the right-hand bend and take the obvious rough track downhill to Chatsworth Road. Keep right and go over the bridge, following signs for the car park. Go through this to a gate and, after the houses, head **NW** up the track for 1.5km, zig-zagging through farm buildings to a gate. Go L through a gate up the wall edge, through the next gate and climb up to Manners Wood. At the top, pass through the double gates and onto the obvious path through the woods. L at the junction after the first steep section and immediately R down the next. At the crossroads, go **SA** then L at the junction, over a slight rise and down fast bends to the main road.

4 R onto *A6* for 2km until Haddon Hall car park, take bridleway L just beyond car park, climb along obvious track then wall and fence edge, through bridlegate by farm building and **SA** along fence. Turn L through gate and follow steep path down technical hairpins to pond, then continue **SA** up small lane towards Youlgreave church. **SA** at crossroads, keep L at next downhill junction, watch out for bridleway hidden behind parked cars on left when road bends right. Drop to cross footbridge, then L along river for 150m and follow lane uphill to R. Bear off R after farmhouse alongside rickety caravans, and take track across fields, across small lane, then obvious track down to river and up other side to B5056.

5 R onto road then L up minor road signposted *Birchover*. Climb through village, and just after village shop turn R down lane. At brow of hill (250m, village stocks opposite), take track L and continue until bottom of steep rutted track. Keep R then immediately L and drop down potholed tarmac lane to join road – keep R downhill to Darley Bridge. Turn L at junction, over bridge to start-finish point.

◄━◖◗━ **Making a day of it**

At 35km this is already a big ride. But if it's not enough, the kilometre just after Calton Lees Farm is shared with the **Bakewell Circuit** (see page 49). Lap this as many times as you feel necessary before continuing.

DESCENDING WIN HILL

Hope Tour – Central Peak

33.3km

Introduction

If anyone was in any doubt about the world-class quality of Peak District mountain biking then this route should settle their minds. Over 30km of fully rideable uphill and downhill action. Simply superb. Starting from Hope, this classy excursion describes a series of rider-friendly loops that take in some of the best terrain that the Peak has to offer.

The Ride

The popular turnpike at Hope Cross is accessed via a great little climb up from the Edale Road. Following the elevated course of the Roman road allows some classic Peak District scenery to be enjoyed, before the steep and loose descent that begins just past Blackley Clough. The riding that follows up past Rowlee Farm is stiff but not too drastic and soon leads past Lockerbrook Farm for a great descent to the banks of Derwent Reservoir. The climb up from here starts out earnestly enough, but stick with it – a concentrated effort will soon see you through the loose stuff before the gradient eases and the track eventually spills you back out onto that wonderful ridge that you just dropped down from. This time the descent is even better – great rocky track leading to a series of quick bends down over the A57 onto the southern banks of Ladybower. An easy-going track, a great forest section and some cunningly linked back roads then lead you (not without effort!) up onto Win Hill for another fast and furious descent to the Edale Road and then back into Hope.

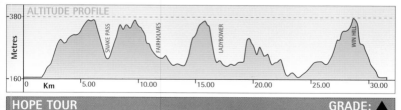

HOPE TOUR	GRADE: ▲
DISTANCE: 33.3KM	**TOTAL ASCENT:** 1,365M
START/FINISH: HOPE	**GRID REFERENCE:** SK 171835
PARKING: HOPE CAR PARK	**CAFÉ:** WOODBINE CAFÉ, HOPE Tel: 07778 113 882
PUBLIC HOUSE: PLENTY TO CHOOSE FROM IN HOPE	

Hope Tour

Directions – Hope Tour

❺ Turn **R** out of Hope car park, taking the first **L** onto Edale Road. Follow this, passing under concrete railway bridge and over River Noe on road bridge – take first **R**, (**SA**) onto Fullwood Stile Lane just past bridge. Continue up tarmac track to gate. Continue **SA** through gate, track becomes stony and more technical. Follow this track as it undulates for approx. 1km (all good stuff). Continue **SA** where a sandy track comes down acutely from the right, through gate, along the course of the Roman road, passing through a gate then up steep little section (choice of flags or singletrack) through next gate to junction at Hope Cross. Continue **SA**.

2 Continue past awkward ford crossing at Blackley Clough, soon descending on loose and tricky ground to gate, turn **R** down metalled track, drop steeply crossing river – climb up to *A57*. Cross busy *A57* with care, continue **SA** up farm track past Rowlee Farm – through gate, well-surfaced track zig-zags up, eventually passing through second gate and on to four-way junction bear **L** to Lockerbrook Farm.

3 Just past farm continue **SA** through gate. A short climb precedes a furious descent leading to a gate and the road – through gate, turn **R** following road to Fairholmes. From Fairholmes continue **SA** along road, passing two large (and some small) car-parking areas on the right. Just past second parking, a bridleway leads up and **R** through gate, just before the cattle grid, steep and loose at first, soon easing to climb through forest.

4 Turn **R** at top, through the gate to join a sandy track descending to the four-way junction passed previously. This time, turn **L** through gate to a steep stony track – a superb descent, one of the best in the Peak. Pass through two more gates and hit the busy A57 – approach and cross this hazardous road with care. **SA** onto steep, stony and often greasy track leading down to bridge. Cross bridge and bear **L** up muddy track to gate, turn **L** and down through gate onto southern bank of Ladybower Reservoir.

5 Follow the shore until a forestry track, signed *Bridleway*, heads steadily up **R**. **SA** at the crossroads where the track levels out, excellent riding, mainly in descent, continuing **SA** where track tantalisingly drops down to a sharp bermed left-hand bend. Follow level track back to join main shoreline track. Follow banks of reservoir until a slight climb takes you up and away before turning south to rejoin the reservoir bank, passing the dam wall on the left.

6 Continue down track, looking out for permitted bridleway on **R** after 250m. Continue **SA** through two gates to meet road, head **R** uphill. On reaching village of Thornhill, take **R** turn just before telephone box – Carr Lane (signposted *Not Suitable for Motors*). Steadily uphill to Aston, look out for **R** turn uphill on tarmac (signposted *Win Hill and Hope Cross*). Uphill to join muddy walled bridleway **L** past Edge Farm. Track levels off slightly, undulating beneath the SW flank of Win Hill. At junction with wide bridleway, descend **L** to join wide sandy track (Roman road).

7 Take an acute **L** here (almost doubling back) for long, fast swoop down the flank of Win Hill – not without interest and mainly in descent – eventually joining farm track at gate. Roll down track bearing **R** onto road (Edale Road). Bear **L** along road, under railway bridge back into Hope – turn **R** to return to car park.

A HANDFUL OF BRAKE PHOTO: JOHN COEFIELD

Hope Valley Circuit – Central Peak   45km

Introduction

Strictly speaking this is mostly on the Dark Peak Map, but a good proportion of the route is on the 'White Stuff'. Basically a really big loop around the Hope Valley, taking in several tough climbs, some fantastic descents and only a smidgen of tarmac. Because of its variety of terrain, naturalness and geography it is a contender for one of the best enduro style rides in the UK.

The Ride

Several starting points are possible, but Hathersage is our favourite, although that does leave the toughest climb until last. Out of the village, height is quickly gained on a quiet lane, then steady singletrack leads up onto the limestone, before a great descent to Bradwell, and a proper long slog up onto the moors above Castleton. Maintaining height, the route swings north towards and then over Mam Tor, before heading back east for the long return leg. Great descending and ascending into and back out of Edale, takes in the best riding the Dark Peak has to offer. A descent from Win Hill brings you back into the Hope Valley. A quick blast drops the tiring rider into Bamford, from where a mean little lane climbs up to the edge of Stanage Moor and the Long Causeway climb up to Stanage Edge. The descent is superb, and a little technical in places, with the finale down the lane back to the village of Hathersage.

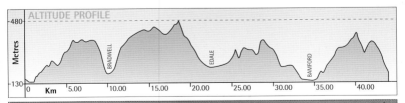

ALTITUDE PROFILE

HOPE VALLEY CIRCUIT	GRADE: ▲
DISTANCE: 45KM	**TOTAL ASCENT:** 1,529M
START/FINISH: HATHERSAGE	**GRID REFERENCE:** SK 231814
PARKING: HATHERSAGE PAY AND DISPLAY	**CAFÉ:** OUTSIDE CAFÉ Tel: 01433 651 936
PUBLIC HOUSE: PLENTY TO CHOOSE FROM IN HATHERSAGE	

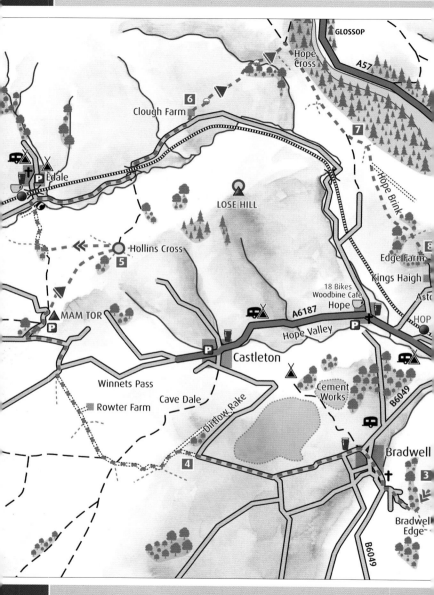

GLOSSOP

Hope Cross

A57

6

Clough Farm

7

Hope Brink

Edale

LOSE HILL

Edge Farm

8

Kings Haigh

Hollins Cross

Asto

5

18 Bikes
Woodbine Café

≪

Hope

HOP

MAM TOR

A6187

Hope Valley

Castleton

Winnets Pass

Cave Dale

Dirtlow Rake

Cement Works

B6049

Rowter Farm

Bradwell

4

Bradwell Edge

3

≪

B6049

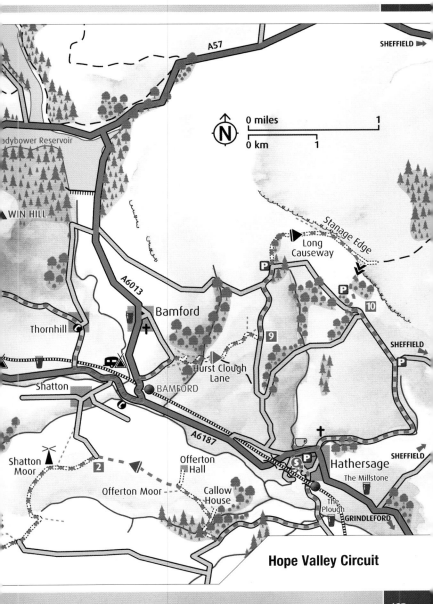

Hope Valley Circuit

Directions – Hope Valley Circuit

6   **R** out of Hathersage swimming pool car park, then **L** heading downhill on the B6001 towards Grindleford. Just after 1km take the tarmac road **R** signed *Gliding Club/ Abney*. Climb up the road for 1.4km branching **R** on the narrow tarmac road just before the farm complex of Highlow Hall on the brow. Follow the narrow road through trees traversing around the valley head, past Callow House. Just before Offerton Hall, at the right-hand bend in the descending lane, go **SA** on the bridleway across moorland. The trail climbs steadily before a short descent to a gate and junction with the road.

2   **L** up road and track past the mast and along the level rutted track onto Shatton Moor. At a rough T-junction head **L** on bridleway following track as it curves round **R** passing footpath coming from the left. Pass roadhead on left, keep **SA** and descend fast, looking out for bridleway signed through gate on **L**. If the track gets steep and rocky you've missed the bridleway sign.

3   Take this across the field and then **L** downhill, on singletrack – superb, eventually emerging into village of Bradwell. Go **R** on main road, through traffic lights, then take the road, Town Lane, **L**, just before the football playing field. Up to the junction, **ignore** bridleway signed straight ahead, turn **L**, and keep **SA** uphill out of the village. Turn **R** at the T-junction, and follow the road as it starts to curve round.

4   **SA** onto a rough quarry track, before the road starts to descend again. Follow this for a few metres, turning **L** up the stony lane of Dirtlow Rake. Keep **SA**, past various old quarries, to a gate. **SA**, keep **SA** at the junction of bridleways (right goes off to the awesome descent of Cave Dale into Castleton), then take the bridletrack **R** at the next junction. Follow this **SA** to reach the main road. Turn **R** and follow the road round, **ignoring** right turns to Winnats Pass and Blue John Cavern. Take the next road **R** up to Mam Tor Gap, just past the large car park on the right. Just over the brow, at a bus-stop take the singletrack **R**, through the gate, and up along the side of Mam Tor, soon in fast descent to the cairn of Hollins Cross.

5   Turn acutely back **L**, and take the excellent fast and sweeping descent down to eventually meet the lane coming up from Edale. Turn **R** onto this lane, and follow it down to the main valley road. Turn **R** and head down the valley. After passing the Youth Hostel and riding school, look out for a gate on the **L**, and bridleway entrance, signed *Footpath and Bridleway to Alport*.

6   Go through the gate, **SA** up walled path. Cross the ford, through the gate and **SA** up a pleasant track through two further gates before **SA** for steep descent to Jaggers Clough – get into low gear before ford and gate. Cross ford through gate, **SA** up steep and loose track, **SA** to junction with Roman road. Turn **R**, down the track.

7   **Ignore** stony track descending **R**, but take the singletracks and ruts off to the **L**, uphill onto the broad shoulder of Win Hill. Keep **SA** for about 500m, looking out for a small cairn on the **R** (**don't** keep following the track – if you get to a gate you've missed the cairn). Take the narrow trail off to the **R**, a fast descent down the flank of Win Hill. Go **SA** through the gate, up to a second gate and **SA** across the field, picking up a prominent track – the muddy lane, down through a couple of gates, to emerge onto tarmac at Edge Farm.

8   Downhill, and **L** at the T-junction, keep **SA** through the village of Aston, and along the narrow road to Thornhill. Turn **R** in the village, down to the main Hope Valley road, where you turn **L** and head up to the traffic lights at Sickleholme Service Station. Turn **L**, over the railway bridge, and take the first **R**, up Saltergate Lane. Turn **R** at the top, and head **SA** along the *Unsuitable for Motors* Hurst Clough Lane. **Ignore** left branch at single bar gate to sewage works, keep **SA** and descend into Hurst Clough, get in low gear (you have been warned) for a shocking climb out on those tiring legs. Keep **SA** on lane, up past the farms and eventually onto the road. Turn **L**.

9   Head up the lane, turning **R** at the T-junction, and keep **SA** onto the lane, just past the cattle-grid, up the ever steepening and increasingly rocky Long Causeway, sometimes rideable, but usually seriously tricky, depending on the rocks. At the summit, follow the track onto the moor, and where the track bears left heading out across to Stanage Pole, turn **R** back down to the edge. Head back on yourself for a few metres and start the descent, with a few very tricky little steps, twists and turns. The trail continues its superb technical descending, nothing horrendous, but requiring concentration throughout. After the third gate, just after emerging from the trees, branch off to the **L**, across the grass and down to the road.

10   Turn **L**, and **L** again at the junction, uphill, turning **R** at the top, over the cattle grid and a rapid descent back into Hathersage, turn **R** onto the main road, then **L** and **L** again into the car park.

Well Done!

Linacre Classic – East Peak

27km

Introduction

Two things stand out about this excellent circuit, firstly there seems to be a lot more down than up – and secondly it has the lowest gates per kilometre of any ride in the Peak – scientifically proven. So on a dry day, with a fresh pair of legs, you can really get some good times for this ride. It is a quiet ride, and the high proportion of quality singletrack makes for an entertaining trip few have experienced. Worth doing in both directions, the described route is all rideable with a few technical bits which will throw off all but the best, whereas the clockwise route has some short sharp climbs, and long satisfying singletrack descents.

The Ride

Starting from the day-trippers' honey pot of Linacre Reservoirs, the route describes a big anti-clockwise circuit around the beautiful eastern edge of the White Peak. The ride rolls with the landscape, up hill and down dale, heading out to the gritstone edges, before dropping back down to farm and woodland trails. Characterised by long steady descents and ascents, a different proposition in the wet, but a great day out in the summer.

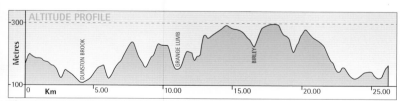

ALTITUDE PROFILE

Metres — 300, 100

Km — 0, 5.00, 10.00, 15.00, 20.00, 25.00

DUNSTON BROOK — GRANGE LUMB — BIRLEY

LINACRE CLASSIC

GRADE: ▲

DISTANCE: 27KM

START/FINISH: LINACRE RESERVOIRS

PARKING: FREE CAR PARK

PUBLIC HOUSE: THE GATE INN, OVERGREEN Tel: 01246 276 923

TOTAL ASCENT: 790M

GRID REFERENCE: SK 334729

CAFÉ: ICE CREAM AT THE RESERVOIRS IF IT'S HOT

continues on
NEXT PAGE

Linacre Classic (Part 1)

continued from
LAST PAGE

Barlow Moor

Grange
Hill

Birle
Gran

Gate
Posts

Birley
Farm

Wigley Hal
Farm

B6050

A619

◄ BASLOW

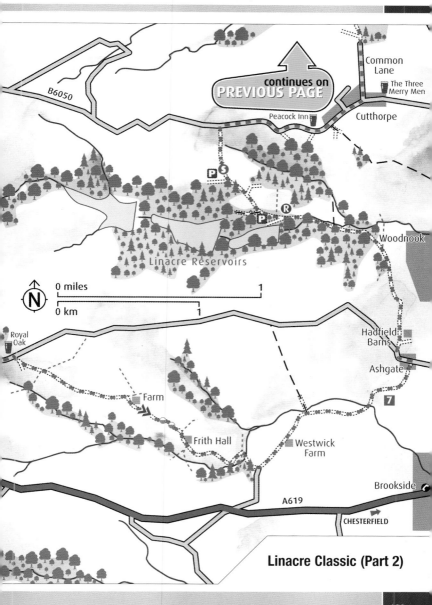

continues on
PREVIOUS PAGE

Common Lane

The Three Merry Men

Cutthorpe

B6050

Peacock Inn

Woodnook

Linacre Reservoirs

0 miles   1

0 km   1

Royal Oak

Hadfield Barns

Ashgate

Farm

Frith Hall

Westwick Farm

Brookside

A619

CHESTERFIELD

Linacre Classic (Part 2)

Directions – Linacre Classic

➊ Exit the car park and head uphill on tarmac back towards the road. Turn **R** dropping into the village of Cutthorpe. Turn **L** at the junction down Common Lane. Head downhill, branching **R** onto a very loose bridleway which drops down to a ford, cross this and head back up to the road. Turn **R** into Barlow then **L** at the junction going **SA** onto Furness Lane, continue **SA** onto Smelting House Lane.

2 At the base of the hill, continue **SA** steeply at first up the signed bridleway, this soon eases into a long steady climb. Turn **L** at the road and drop down, looking out for a track off **L** on the corner – signed *Unsuitable for Motors*. Take this excellent little descent, emerging once again onto the road. Turn **R** at the T-junction, taking the signed bridleway on the **R** after a few metres.

3 Follow this excellent singletrack, always steady but always uphill. Turn **L** at the road, descending to pass one bus stop, and taking the bridleway **R** at the second bus stop. Tricky at first across a boggy ford, and then great climbing up singletrack. The track turns to a stream, you are cycling on exposed bedrock, and the vegetation closes in around you – is this the source of the Amazon? This climb will beat all but the most dedicated. Look out for a handy alternative exit **R**, follow an easier pleasant farm track up to the road.

4 Head downhill once again, taking a bridleway **L** just after Horsley Gate on the right. Head **R** at the road, then take the **L** fork climbing uphill for some way before a good track leads off **R**, just opposite a farm – signed *Bridleway to Baslow Road*. Head downhill, fork **R** into the woods, taking a bridleway through a gate to the **L**. Cross the tricky ford, then yet more steady singletrack climbing, to emerge onto a road. Head **SA**, passing a road to the left and then one to the right, down past various farms and houses, before taking the lane off to the **R**, signed *Spitewinter Lane*.

5 Descend gingerly on the unconsolidated surface, branching off **L** just before the buildings of Bank Farm. Cross the stream and head back uphill to the road. Turn **L**. Head **SA** down the road, keeping **SA** to eventually take a **R** turn down a good lane, just after a road on the left. Descend past various houses, and past Birley Grange, to take the signed bridleway through the woods – emerging onto a tarmac bridleway, by a second pond. Turn **L** and head **SA** through some impressive gates, dropping down to Birley Farm. Turn **R** at the farm entrance and head down across the grass to pick up a fine singletrack descent.

6　Keep **SA**, descent soon turns to ascent, with hard riding, particularly in the wet, to thankfully reach the road. It's all downhill from here. Turn **L** onto the road, and head to the pub, taking the track opposite for a fast descent to a farm. Swing **R** at the farm entrance, on the Chesterfield Round Walk, great descending to some fords, and then a steady climb out to a road head. I know I said it was all downhill, I meant to say mostly. Head **L** at the road head, down the lane. Keep **SA**, **ignoring** a nice looking bridleway off to the left.

7　Head up to the road, and turn **L**, round the bend, taking the signed bridleway, a good track off to the **R**, passing the glorious looking Hadfield Barns. Descend into the woods, keeping **SA**, passing the ranger station, and then **SA** back up to the car. Or if you're feeling fresh, head off into the woods on one of the marked bridleway trails.

← Making a day of it

The **Linacre Classic** is a fair old distance as it stands. However, if you're a bit of a fitness fanatic, you could extend it into the **Holymoorside** loop (see page 85) near Wigley (**GR SK 315717**), returning to the **Classic** near Westwick Farm (**GR SK 337707**).

THE NOTORIOUS WIGLEY HILL

ABOVE BAKEWELL

Rowsley Circuit – Central Peak

Introduction

Another big old circle of mountain biking fun. Centred in the heart of the White Peak, it has plenty of ups and downs, lots of singletrack, and while challenging, is a good introduction to longer routes, especially when the trails are dry.

The Ride

From Rowsley steady climbing gives way to tough climbing on fantastic trails leading onto the Duke of Devonshire's front garden. From the village of Edensor the route climbs up and then descends with speed and fun down to Bakewell, crosses the Wye and over the farmland pastures of Haddon to a delightful, skill-testing descent to Lathkill Dale. Passing through the villages of Youlgreave and Birchover, on great, varied, terrain, the final descent is a fitting finale to this fine ride.

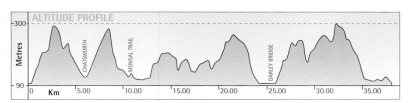

ALTITUDE PROFILE

CHATSWORTH MONSAL TRAIL DARLEY BRIDGE

Metres · 300 · 90

Km 0 5.00 10.00 15.00 20.00 25.00 30.00 35.00

ROWSLEY CIRCUIT   GRADE: ▲

DISTANCE: 38.5KM

START/FINISH: ROWSLEY

PARKING: ROWSLEY CAR PARK

PUBLIC HOUSE: THE FARMYARD INN, YOULGREAVE Tel: 01629 636 211

TOTAL ASCENT: 1,170M

GRID REFERENCE: SK 257659

CAFÉ: HAVE A LOOK IN BAKEWELL!

Edensor

PO

Edensor
Tea Rooms

3

Ballcross
Farm

Golf
Course

Monsal Trail

2

Bakewell

A619

B6048

A6(t)

4

Haddon
Hall

Chu
La

Nutseats
Quarry

B5056

**continues on
NEXT PAGE**

FB

Youlgreave

5

**Rowsley Circuit
(Part 1)**

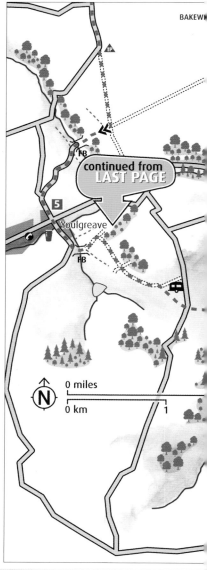

BAKEW

continued from LAST PAGE

5

Youlgreave

0 miles

0 km   1

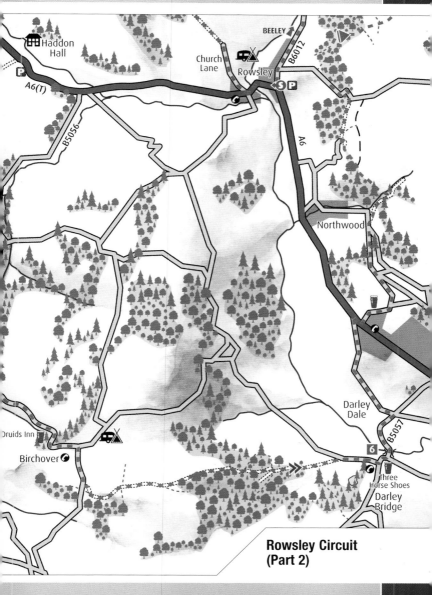

**Rowsley Circuit
(Part 2)**

Directions – Rowsley Circuit

⊙➤ From the car park, head west, on the A6 (direction Bakewell) for a short distance, taking the first **R**, up Church Lane, follow this **SA** to where it gives up its tarmac and heads off into the Peak, traversing through woodland, to reach a crossroads, **ignore** the tracks off to the left and straight ahead, but go through the gate on the **R** and up the dirt singletrack into the woods. Superb hard, but rideable climbing through the trees. You emerge onto a level piece of track, but after a short few metres, breath recovered, branch off **R** uphill once again. The track levels off, onto fast and boggy woodland singletrack which twists and turns to a gate.

2 Through the double gates and downhill, fast and furious, to the woods and another gate, go **R** down the trail (**not SA**) and take the **L** fork where the bridleway splits. Follow the track up across the field and into the woods. **SA** through the woods. Where the track emerges, go **SA** down the parkland, watch those jumps! Aiming for a small clump of trees. Finger-posts mark the way. Turn **R** just before the trees and keep going across the Devonshires' front lawn towards the road.

3 **L** down the road, soon branching off to the **L** onto a signed bridleway, back onto the road, then **L** signed *Edensor Tea Rooms*. **SA** keeping the church to your left. Up the road, then track, a good honest climb, go **SA** on the road at the top. Just beyond the brow of the hill, and immediately after a farm track on the left, before Ballcross Farm on the right, take the bridleway steeply down into the trees. Superb classic MTB descending brings one to the golf course, cross this (**danger** – imagine the embarrassment of being hit). Drop onto the Monsal Trail, heading **L**, to where it ends. Turn off the trail, **ignore** the tarmac and drop down into the fields towards the river. Follow the bridleway as it weaves along the valley floor, before exiting onto a metalled road.

4 Turn **R** and follow the road onto the main A6, turn **R** and head along the busy road for 750m to the edge of Bakewell. Take the lane off to the **L** – Intake Lane. Follow this deteriorating into a field to soon meet another road. **L** and after 500m, at the bend in the road, go **SA** through the gate onto the farm track. Follow the track towards farm buildings. Just before the buildings, turn **R**, through the gate, along the side of the field. Turn **L** through gate and follow steep path down hairpins to a pond, then continue **SA** up the small lane towards Youlgreave church.

5 **SA** at crossroads, keep **L** at next downhill junction, watch out for bridleway hidden behind parked cars on **L** when road bends right. Drop to cross footbridge, then **L** along river 150m and follow lane uphill to **R**. Bear off **R** after farmhouse alongside rickety caravans, and take the track across fields, across a small lane, then down obvious track to the river and up the other side to the B5056. **R** onto road then **L** up minor road signposted *Birchover*. Climb through village, and just after village shop turn **R** down lane. At brow of hill (250m, village stocks opposite), take track **L** and continue until bottom of steep rutted track. Keep **R** then immediately **L** and drop down potholed tarmac lane to join road – keep **R** to downhill Darley Bridge.

6 Turn **L** at the T-junction and follow the road, crossing the river, take the first **L**, 300m after the bridge. Follow this road to where it joins the A6, **R** then first **L** climbing out of the valley. Keep on this road, **ignoring** three minor roads off to the **R**, take the **fourth**, that being the small lane to the **R**, 100m before the road turns left and starts to descend again. Follow this lane, turning up **R** onto the bridletrack before the corner. Head uphill, looking out for the bridleway off to the **L** just before the edge of the woods. Follow this contouring bridleway through woods, passing through two gates where a track intersects. At the road, descend via two hairpins and take farm track **R** just after house, climbing for 200m until bridleway drops **L** into woods, then climbs sharply to a wooden bridge. Turn sharp **R** after the bridge and climb via a gate into fields, taking the farm track between buildings heading **NE**. Join road after 1.5km, **R** onto Beeley Hill for 1km, then keep **L** on right-hand bend and take obvious rough track downhill to Chatsworth Road.

7 Turn **L** and follow road (B6012) back to Rowsley.

←⊂∞⊃ Making a day of it

One for the rock climbers out there – this route circles Stanton Moor (**GR SK 244627**), runs right by Eagle Tor and Rowtor (roughly **GR SK 241627**) and isn't a million miles away from Robin Hood's Stride and Cratcliffe (again, roughly **GR SK 223622**) – two of our favourite places in the Peak. Our **Peak District Bouldering** guide includes them all as does **Day Walks in the Peak District**.

THREE SHIRES HEAD

Wildboarclough – West Peak

32km

Introduction

Is it a good ride? Maybe you should be the judge of that. The first half hour or so is excellent – good solid mountain biking, and then it starts to go downhill, or rather uphill. The climb out of Three Shires Head is good and technical, and is not without interest and, unfortunately, a little pushing. The bad news is, that is pretty much it. You still have lots of miles to go, but it is mostly on tarmac and hardpack forest paths.

So why? Well the loop is varied, the scenery is stunning, the Macc Forest loop is great, I've seen heaps of wildlife on the route and the legs certainly know you've had a good ride. It is also a good winter loop, with only the section from Three Shires Head to Flash proving sticky.

The Ride

Descending to the Three Shires Head, the ride then traverses to the by-road out of Flash. It then climbs over Midgley Hill, before entering the quiet lanes through Wildboarclough, and up to the edge of Macclesfield Forest. On a clear day the tremendous descent and massive climb back out can be seen clearly, as can the final road climb back up to the Cat and Fiddle.

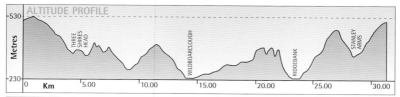

ALTITUDE PROFILE

Metres — 530 / 230 — Km — THREE SHIRES HEAD — WILDBOARCLOUGH — RIDGEBANK — STANLEY ARMS — 0 | 5.00 | 10.00 | 15.00 | 20.00 | 25.00 | 30.00

WILDBOARCLOUGH

GRADE: ▲

DISTANCE: 32KM

START/FINISH: CAT AND FIDDLE

PARKING: LAY-BY OPPOSITE THE PUB ON A537

PUBLIC HOUSE: CAT AND FIDDLE Tel: 01298 23 364

TOTAL ASCENT: 1,150M

GRID REFERENCE: SK 001719

CAFÉ: FIVEWAYS CAFÉ, JUNCTION OF DALE ROAD/LONDON ROAD/HIGH STREET Tel: 01298 72 018

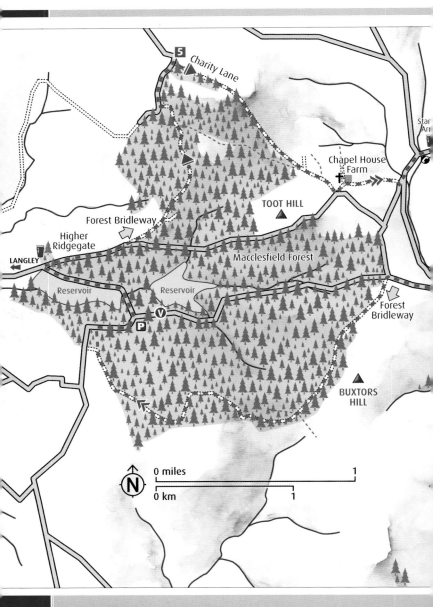

MACCLESFIELD

A537

Peak View

Cat & Fiddle

P
S

High Ash
Farm

BUXTON

BUXTON

Danebower
Hollow

A54

Clough
House

continues on
NEXT PAGE

LEEK

**Wildboarclough
(Part 1)**

continues on
PREVIOUS PAGE

0 miles 1

0 km 1

Wildboarclough

4

CONGLETON

Heild End
Farm

TAGSC
H

Allgreave

MIDGLEY HILL

continued from
LAST PAGE

BUXTON

A54

Farm

Three Shires
Head

2

3

Manor
Farm

**Wildboarclough
(Part 2)**

Directions – Wildboarclough

➏➤ Park in the lay-by opposite the Cat and Fiddle Pub, and take the good bridleway, through the gate, heading south, straight across the moor. Follow this **SA** to its end, exiting onto the busy road. Turn **R**, and head downhill for approximately 500m looking out for a tarmac farm track, signed *Bridleway*, off to the left. Turn **L** here and descend towards the farm. Turn **R** up the fenced track, just on the apex of the bend, before the farm. Go through the gate and **SA** down the track, then head **L** and pick up a stream, and more defined tracks, turning **R** at the wall, **don't** go through the gate. The track descends to the stream. Descend with fun to the footbridge at the Three Shires Head.

2 Cross the bridge, turn **R** and steady climbing takes you away from the stream. The climb steepens before contouring around the hill and the track turns to tarmac at some houses. Follow this past the scramble bikes' playground, looking out for a signed bridleway on the **R**. Take this, a challenging descent, to a ford and an equally challenging (push) up to a rideable path, some llamas, and a paved section to the road.

3 Turn **R** and race down the road, to a T-junction, turn **R** again, and follow the road, down into the valley and then steeply back out the other side. Follow the hill to its apex and look out for a bridleway on the **R**, just after a barn, and before a house. Take this track, soon easing to climb over Midgley Hill. Descend to the road. Turn **L** and descend to the valley bottom, just after a big sweeping hairpin, climb up the other side a short distance, turning **R** to Wildboarclough.

4 Leaving the village follow the meandering valley bottom lane for several kilometres, taking the lane on the **L**, signed *Langley, A Quiet Lane*. A very steep tarmac climb up to the summit at the edge of the forest. At the crest, turn **L** onto the forest bridleway, a good hardpack trail which undulates through the woods, before a very fast descent down to the road, keep following the bridleway signs which lead down to and along the side of the reservoir, to a pub! And then **R** and then forking **L** back onto forest trails, for a long climb back up to the road. Turn **R** on the road, and climb up the steepest part of the climb, to a track leading off **R** just before the road turns sharp left.

5 Take this track, a bit of a grind, to the summit, before a good descent down to Chapel House Farm. Turn **L** towards the chapel, and then turn **R** down *Unsuitable for Cars and Bikes*, but suitable for loose packed steep descending specialists. Steep sliding fun to the road. Follow the signs and the incline to Buxton. First **L**, to the Stanley Arms, then **R** to climb up to the Cat and Fiddle Road, then **R** back to the start.

◄●▭ Making a day of it

From the start, head out along the main road, take the track over Axe Edge Moor (take a map for directions) and make your way over to the **South Buxton** ride (see page 97) just over the A53 (**GR SK 039695**). Ride this in reverse to the Traveller's Rest pub (**GR SK 032678**) and nip down the road through the village of Flash to rejoin the original ride (**GR SK 018669**).

SECTION 4

Bonus Section

Done all the rides day and night, winter and summer, linked them all together? Traversed the Peak North to South, East to West? Well what more can we offer? I'm afraid it's either taking the kids out on one of our Family Rides or forgetting about being able to have kids, and tackling the Hollinsclough descents.

Bonus Section
sponsored by

www.ibiscycles.com

Rides FAMILY

Hills, rocks and children don't always mix. Kids might have a real affinity for mud, but on the whole, the majority of the routes in this book probably aren't the sort of rides you might take your family on. So if you've decided, in the spirit of self-sacrifice, that your day's riding will be spent with the kids, (or if you've taken the decision to train them up early), we've included a few rides that are suitable to help you out. Of course, they're also good for an easy day out, or for introducing friends to mountain biking. See also Vertebrate Publishing's **Cycling in the Peak District.**

Carsington Water

Distance:	13km circuit around a reservoir
Map:	OS OL24; A free route map is available from the visitor centre
Starting Point:	Carsington Water Visitor Centre
Grid Reference:	SK 241517
Car Parking:	Pay and Display at the Visitor Centre
Cycle Hire:	Carsington Water Visitor Centre, Tel: 01629 540 478
Visitor Centre:	Carsington Water, www.carsingtonwater.com, Tel: 01629 540 696

A popular little circuit around Britain's ninth largest reservoir, this is a relatively hilly route that should leave most novices feeling as though they've been on a pretty tough ride. Starting from the visitor centre, the trail circles the reservoir, passing through carefully managed woodland and the stone-built village of Hopton, where you can take a break at the local pub if you need it.

Back at the visitor centre, there's a large adventure playground, a designated barbeque area and opportunities to go horse riding, sailing and canoeing. The centre itself houses a permanent exhibition, explaining the role of water in our lives and a café and souvenir shop. The site was awarded a 'Forestry Centre of Excellence' for its management of the local woodland, which is home to a wide variety of wildlife, most notably the birds who reside at the reservoir. You can watch them from two purpose-built hides and from the conservation area on the far side of the lake. Don't leave without a look at the Kugel Stone in the centre of the courtyard. This ball of granite weighs over a tonne and sits on a thin layer of water under pressure, allowing you to move it with the touch of your hand.

High Peak Trail

Distance:	Up to 28km each way along a disused railway path
Map:	OS OL24
Starting Point:	This trail can be started from the north at Parsley Hay, the High Peak Junction at the south or Middleton Top Visitor Centre, about two thirds of the way down the trail
Grid Reference:	Parsley Hay: SK 147637, High Peak Junction: SK 315561, Middleton Top: SK 276552
Car Parking:	There is a pay and display car park at Parsley Hay, and parking is also available at Middleton Top and High Peak Junction
Cycle Hire:	Middleton Top Cycle Hire Centre, Tel: 01629 823 204 Parsley Hay, Tel: 01298 84 493
Visitor Centres:	Middleton Top Visitor Centre, Tel: 01629 823 204 Parsley Hay, Tel: 01298 84 493

A well-known route, the High Peak Trail follows the course of the old Cromford and High Peak Railway which, completed in 1830, was among the earliest in the country. It runs from Parsley Hay at its north end down to Cromford Canal in the south, and is probably most easily ridden as a 'there-and-back' route. It's worth pointing out that the trail does literally run down from north to south, with the steepest sections at the southern end and you should bear this in mind when deciding how far along the route you wish to ride. Unlike many railway routes, the High Peak Trail twists and turns surprisingly sharply as it runs through the limestone scenery of the White Peak, so the view changes regularly. Back at Parsley Hay, the trail meets the Tissington Trail, so you can always head off down this if you're still feeling lively.

Middleton Top, about two thirds of the way down the trail, sits at the top of the Middleton incline and houses a steam winding engine, built in 1892, to haul wagons up and down the incline. It can be seen running on the first weekend of each month in the summer and on bank holidays. Further south, near to High Peak Junction, is the Cromford Canal, where several remnants of the area's historical importance as an industrial centre are still maintained as part of the Derwent Valley Mills World Heritage Site.

Monsal Trail

Distance:	Up to 8km each way along a disused railway path
Map:	OS OL24; A map is available for 50p from Bakewell Cycle Hire
Starting Point:	Bakewell Cycle Hire
Grid Reference:	SK 223690
Car Parking:	Bakewell
Cycle Hire:	Bakewell Cycle Hire, Tel: 01335 348 603
Visitor Centres:	None for the trail itself, but Bakewell has a Tourist Information Centre, Tel: 01629 813 227

Following the line of the old Midland Railway through the centre of the Peak District, the full Monsal Trail is around 14.4km long, but only a short section, from Bakewell to Monsal Head, is suitable for cyclists. Even so, it's worthwhile – you're on your bike and you're passing through some lovely scenery. A nice little ride that shouldn't take too long to complete, it would also be a shame to turn back at Little Longstone without a quick trip down the road to Monsal Head, where you can look down Monsal Dale at one of the best views in the Peak.

The remainder of the route burrows its way through the hills towards Buxton, with high maintenance costs forcing the closure of the many tunnels along the route, although walkers can bypass them on footpaths. The full railway line was completed in the 1860s, linking Manchester with London. Bakewell station was used to receive coal from remote areas, and to dispatch milk from local farms to the cities. The line was eventually closed just over a century later and bought by the Peak National Park Authority, who opened it as a cycle trail in 1980.

Tissington Trail

Distance:	Up to 21km each way along a disused railway
Map:	Landranger 119, OS OL24
Starting Points:	Ashbourne Cycle Hire, Parsley Hay
Grid Reference:	Ashbourne Cycle Hire: SK 174468, Parsley Hay: SK 147637
Car Parking:	There is a pay and display car park at Parsley Hay; Ashbourne
Cycle Hire:	Ashbourne Cycle Hire, Tel: 01335 343 156; Parsley Hay, Tel: 01298 84 493
Visitor Centres:	Parsley Hay, Tel: 01298 84 493; Ashbourne Tourist Information, Tel: 01335 343 666

The Tissington Trail is another well-known route that follows the tracks of a disused railway line. As with the High Peak Trail, there is a gentle drop as the trail runs south; nothing too severe but a possible consideration when planning a ride. (Tackle the hill with fresh legs from the south and kids will have forgotten all about the climb by the time they've free-wheeled most of the way back to the car!) This time, the former railway was the Ashbourne to Buxton line, completed in 1899 and closed in 1967. Four years later it then became one of the first lines to be re-opened as a recreational trail.

The Tissington Trail meets both the High Peak Trail and the Pennine Bridleway at Parsley Hay, so there's nothing stopping you linking them. A technically easy but long ride starts at Ashbourne, climbs the Tissington Trail to Parsley Hay and then drops down the High Peak Trail until it hits the B5056, which it then follows back into Ashbourne.

Bridleway

Pennine Bridleway

Distance:	Up to around 560km each way (!)
Map:	Harvey Pennine Bridleway Route Map
Website:	www.nationaltrail.co.uk/PennineBridleway

More rugged and wild than some of the other trails described here, the full Pennine Bridleway would take around two weeks to ride (there's a challenge if ever I heard one). Fully signposted throughout its length, the Pennine Bridleway is the first purpose-built long-distance bridleway in Britain, linking the High Peak Trail to Byrness in Northumberland. The idea was initially conceived by Lady Mary Towneley, a keen horse rider, who campaigned for a long-distance route over the Pennines for riders for many years until her death in February 2001.

Beginning on the High Peak Trail near Matlock, it follows the old Cromford and High Peak Railway through the limestone valleys of the White Peak and then turns up onto the Packhorse Road – the first of many packhorse trails along the way – which it follows from Tideswell across the moorland of the Dark Peak to Hayfield. Leaving Derbyshire, it picks its way between moors and reservoirs as it runs north to meet the 75.2km 'Mary Towneley Loop' in Lancashire and North Yorkshire. The loop is a popular ride in its own right and a tough challenge to complete in a day. Leaving the loop, the trail heads on for another 224km through Cumbria and Northumberland National Park to reach its conclusion (or start) in Byrness, Northumberland.

Descents

⚠ Warning Serious Hardcore Descents

While the Peak is overflowing with good hills to throw yourself down, there is perhaps no greater concentration of seriously hardcore, technical trials skill descents than around the village of Hollinsclough in the White Peak. There are several fast downhills, but the character of these bad boys is more intensive, big drop rock steps. Armour is probably a good idea.

1 Tenterhill from Golling Gate

A do-able rock step descent to the ford over the River Dove – good stuff.

2 Tenterhill from Booth Farm

Can be ridden fast, steepening all the time to the ford on the Dove – easy stuff.

3 Hollinsclough Rake

Singletrack with a mega finish down to the ford.

4 & 5 Hollinsclough Moor to Hollinsclough

Two routes down, both are very hardcore, with perhaps the route down from Coatestown being the Big Daddy.

HOLLINSCLOUGH DESCENTS   GRADE: ▲▲

START/FINISH: HOLLINSCLOUGH, FROM WHERE ALL THE HILLS ARE A SHORT RIDE AWAY
GRID REFERENCE: SK 066666 (YES REALLY!)   **PARKING:** LIMITED PARKING IN THE VILLAGE
CAFÉ: NOTHING LOCAL, BRING SANDWICHES   **PUBLIC HOUSE:** THE QUIET WOMAN,
                                                      EARL STERNDALE Tel: 01246 277 271

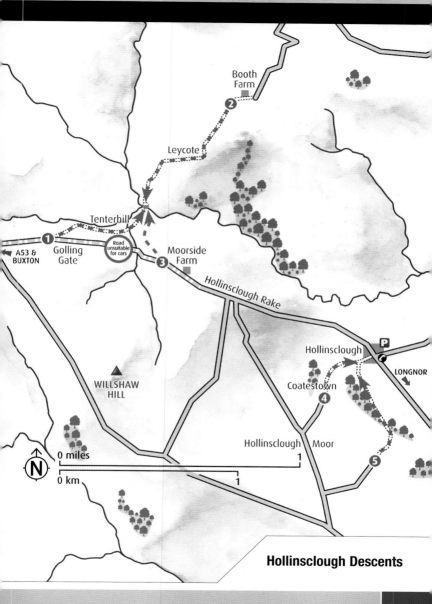

Booth Farm

Leycote

Tenterhill

1 Golling Gate

← A53 & BUXTON

Road unsuitable for cars

3 Moorside Farm

Hollinsclough Rake

▲ WILLSHAW HILL

P Hollinsclough

Coatestown **4**

LONGNOR

Hollinsclough Moor

5

N

0 miles 1

0 km 1

Hollinsclough Descents

In no particular order we have some descents for you to look out for. All good fun, and enough of a challenge to get the pulse racing and the brakes burning.

1 Great Longstone Edge to Rowland   GR SK 215735

Good limestone cobbles and rocks, not super-technical but requires ample concentration and good luck in the wet.

2 Brushfield to Monsal Head   GR SK 175717

A big hill, with sustained descending which just keeps getting steeper, with a nasty twist to drop onto the disused railway line.

3 Golf Course Hill, Bakewell   GR SK 228694

Brilliant woodland singletrack leads to a fast blast across the golf course, down to the Monsal Trail. Not too technical, so just let yourself go and trust those tyres.

4 Manners Wood   GR SK 244678

More brilliant woodland trails, nothing technical, just high-speed fun.

5 Macclesfield Forest – Northern Descent from Charity Lane   GR SJ 967728

About 250 metres of fast descent. Although no natural trails, it is a very fast drop, from the summit of Charity Lane, heading due north onto the road, then south into the forest, and down, down, down to the reservoir. Watch out for ramblers, and indeed bikes toiling up the penultimate hill on the Wildboarclough Circuit.

6 Wormhill to Monk's Dale   GR SK 121746

Up out of Wormhill, then a great little descent – all rocky fun – leads down to the opening of Monk's Dale. Lots of great descents exist in this area. It is impossible to pick any one out, but dropping into Cheedale at Great Rocks Dale, either from the north or south, and the descent of the Limestone Way to Monk's Dale Farm are all superb.

7 Haddon to Youlgreave   GR SK 215652

The Alps come to the White Peak! Albeit short-lived, this series of tight, rocky, technical switchbacks will leave you grinning like a cat from Cheshire. There's nothing else for it – book those flights!

8 Wigley Hill   GR SK 316720

Fast action-packed wooded singletrack fun. An absolutely brilliant descent in the dry! You need to pay attention because there are a few surprises lurking in the undergrowth.

So you think you can climb. On roots? OK – not too bad? Mud? Slippery limestone? All three at once? Remember – no dabs now...

1 Intake Rd
GR SK 298568
Such a fantastic woodland trail, you'll hardly notice you are going uphill. Steep on the tarmac start, but once in the woods enjoy easy ground, tranquillity and remnants of the industrial revolution.

2 Peakley Hill
GR SK 334761
A good, easy, steady climb, though typical White Peak terrain. The trail surface is good, and although steep in places there are no testing bits. You'll arrive refreshed at the top.

3 Pilsley Lane
GR SK 234713
A good little challenge, steep in places and rutted elsewhere. It is short enough to be manageable, but keep up the concentration.

4 Holy Moor Hill
GR SK 329682
A good hill to do – a couple of little technical challenges at the start, but easing all the way. Another of those rare singletrack climbs, with great rewarding riding on the descent back down to Wellspring Farm.

5 Sydnope Hill
GR SK 284632
A big lung buster – hard at the start, especially after rain when the trail gets washed out. Not helped by the steep road out of Darley Dale that makes a good warm up! Anyway the best will cruise the rocky start and sprint on to the top. The rest of us may need a bit of grit to make it.

6 Monsal Head
GR SK 183718
The big daddy of White Peak climbs – steep and long, not technical, just plain hard work. I'd like to say it eases towards the top, but it doesn't. There is ample traction in the dry, which just makes failure more frustrating. The victorious can retire to the Monsal Head Pub and sit on the veranda with a pint, admiring the view, before tackling the true climb – from the viaduct, rather than the cottages.

7 Brough Lane
GR SK 184825
A classic limestone lane, steep and rocky. It starts okay, steep but granny-ringable and on tarmac. Take a quick breather at the farm and bash on up over the rocks. Still steep, the good line at the start disappears as the lane bends to the right. Keep spinning, if you can, and it's soon over as the angle eases and the surface improves.

8 Amber Valley Challenge
GR SK 348628
Another tough climb – only for the best. After leaving Ashover, the trail drops to the River Amber, then rears up, steep and hard, only easing off at Overton Hall. You'll probably need specialist climbing tyres, inflated appropriately on a lightweight rig – and a huge set of lungs and legs.

The White Peak is home to real singletrack fun; it has it all from high moorland narrow ripples through the heather, to super-fast woodland fun. Best served in the dry and when the vegetation has been cut back.

1 Baslow Edge   GR SK 258740

Quite technical, and in a great setting, the trail drops down from the edge, and then picks its way back towards the road. Lots of blocks, streams and bomb-holes to navigate.

2 Black Harry Gate to Bleaklow   GR SK 207742

A rising trail, in a great setting, great fun in either direction. Worth it for the views down Coombs Dale alone.

3 Harewood Grange Farm   GR SK 311679

A superb bit of pristine moorland singletrack, snaking across the heath. It unfortunately comes to an end all too soon.

4 The Amber Valley   GR SK 350627

A sweet bit of twisty trail, running alongside the river, just perfect. Many of the trails in the area are made up of ancient flagstones, but this is the 100% natural hardpack.

5 Northwood   GR SK 270648

If you like your woodland singletrack, and you don't mind belting along trails then come on in, obviously like much of the Peak District woodland it benefits from a bit of dry weather. Bring your best smile.

6 Peakley Hill   GR SK 323773

Strictly speaking a great descent on mega singletrack, it kind of starts a bit wide, then narrows down nicely, to swoopy fun – simply superb.

7 Longdale   GR SK 205592

A great little descent into this fine dry valley, then a pleasant blast along the trail leads to a steady climb out, all on quintessential mountain bike trails.

8 The Woods   GR SK 242679

Around the Chatsworth estate are a lot of great woodland trails – this trail is fortunately legal for us riders, quite short lived but great fun, and only a taste of what is on offer in the White Peak.

Appendices

Tourist Information Centres

Castleton	Tel: 01433 620679
Bakewell	Tel: 01629 813227
Buxton	Tel: 01298 251 06
Glossop	Tel: 01457 855920
Matlock	Tel: 01629 583388

Bike shops
(loads more in the surrounding towns)

Buxton: Mark Anthony Cycles,
115 Spring Gardens
Tel: 01298 72 114

Matlock: Stanley Fearns,
19 Bakewell Rd
Tel: 01629 582089

Whaley Bridge: The Bike Factory,
Beech Road
Tel: 01663 735020

Hope: 18 Bikes,
8 Castleton Road
Tel: 01433 621111

New Mills: Sett Valley Cycles,
9 Union Road, New Mills,
High Peak
Tel: 01663 742629

Bike Hire

Carsington Water Visitor Centre
Tel: 01629 540478

Middleton Top Cycle Hire Centre
Tel: 01629 823204

Parsley Hay
Tel: 01298 84 493

Food and Drink

Cafes
(loads more in surrounding towns and villages)
Woodbine Café, Hope
Tel: 07778 113882

Outside Café, Hathersage
Tel: 01433 651936

Outside Café, Calver Crossroads
Tel: 01433 631111

The Bakewell Pudding Parlour
Tel: 01629 815107

Eyam Tea Rooms, Eyam
Tel: 01433 630725

Elton Café, Elton
Tel: 01629 650217

Pubs

(loads more in surrounding towns and villages)

Bull's Head, Monyash
Tel: 01629 812372

The Druid Inn, Birchover
Tel: 01629 650302

The Red Lion, Litton
Tel: 01298 871458

The Quiet Woman, Earl Sterndale
Tel: 01298 83 211

Three Stags Head, Wardlow Mires
Tel: 01298 872268

Old Sun Inn, Buxton
Tel: 01298 23 452

The Monsal Head Hotel, Monsal Head
Tel: 01629 640250

Weather

www.bbc.co.uk/weather
www.metoffice.com

Accommodation

It's beyond the remit of this guide to give you
a full run-down of tourist accommodation in
the Peak. Here are a few places that have been
recommended to us, but, being local, we haven't
always had direct experience of them ourselves.

Youth Hostels

YHA Bakewell	Tel: 0870 770 5682
YHA Hathersage	Tel: 0870 770 5852
YHA Matlock	Tel: 0870 770 5960

Go to: www.yha.org.uk for more information.

Hotels, Self Catering & B&B

Your best option is probably to look on
www.peakdistrictonline.co.uk or
www.peakdistrict-nationalpark.com.

The Woodbine Café and B&B
Tel: 07778 113882

Campsites

(loads more in the Peak District)

North Lees, Hathersage
Tel: 01433 650838

Eric Byne, Baslow
Tel: 01246 582277

Other Publications

Maps:

Harvey Superwalker – Dark Peak
Harvey Pennine Bridleway Map
OS Explorer OL24 – The Peak District, White Peak Area
OS Explorer OL1 – The Peak District, Dark Peak Area
OS Landranger 119 – Buxton and Matlock

Mountain Bike Guides:

Dark Peak Mountain Biking – True Grit Trails
Paul Evans and Jon Barton, Vertebrate Publishing

Cycling in the Peak District
Jon Barton and Tom Fenton, Vertebrate Publishing

Mountain Biking Trail Centres – The Guide
Tom Fenton, Vertebrate Publishing

Vertebrate Publishing

Vertebrate Publishing (VP) is the imprint of Vertebrate Graphics (VG), Britain's leading graphic design agency that specialises in the outdoor leisure market. Based deliberately near the Peak District, the guidebook production team spends as much time as they can walking, riding and climbing in the Peak District. We have had substantial success in the design and production of specialist outdoor books. These include *Hill Walking – The Official Handbook of the Mountain Leader and Walking Group Leader Schemes* (a bestselling outdoor title for three years running), highly praised rock climbing guidebooks such as *The Roaches – Staffordshire Grit* and the UK's best selling mountain bike guide: *Dark Peak Mountain Biking – True Grit Trails*.

VG create exciting graphic and web design and produce printed literature, advertising and websites, for more details of our services please refer to our website at: **www.v-graphics.co.uk** or e-mail us at: **info@v-graphics.co.uk**

Jon Barton

Jon lives in the heart of the Peak District, married, with a young son. Having climbed and ridden in the area for over a decade his knowledge of the Peak is enviable. After the fame that came from being the best selling author of **Dark Peak Mountain Biking**, Jon has had to improve his MTB skills somewhat. Now proficient at singletrack and merely nervous of descents, his ambition remains to clean the ascent from Gores Farm, Ladybower, where he is available most weekends for book signings, usually spinning out at the first bend. Don't be put off by the cursing – he's really approachable, and surprisingly down to earth.

Andy Heading

Back in the 1980s, Andy's first MTB excursion (on a shiny black Saracen!) was this guidebook's Ashover loop – a circuit around his home village with younger brother Steve. Since then, he's ventured a bit further from home – including 1,097 miles across Alaska to win the Iditasport Impossible winter enduro – but still lives in the White Peak. He is currently official photographer to the European Athletic Association, and also contributes to UK cycling and outdoor magazines.

Mountain Biking Guidebooks from

Our critically acclaimed, comprehensive series of mountain biking guides is the country's bestselling and most respected, purpose-built for the modern mountain biker. Written by riders for riders, our guides are designed to maximise rideability and are full of useful local area information.

Each guidebook features up to 28 rides, complete with comprehensive directions, specialist mapping and inspiring photography, all in a pocket-sized, portable format. The routes are also available on CD, with each route set up in PDF format to allow you to print off just the route you're going to ride and leave the book in the car or at home.

1 Lake District Mountain Biking
Essential Trails

2 Yorkshire Dales Mountain Biking
The North Dales

3 Yorkshire Dales Mountain Biking
The South Dales

4 North York Moors Mountain Biking
Moorland Trails

5 Dark Peak Mountain Biking
True Grit Trails

6 White Peak Mountain Biking
The Pure Trails

7 South West Mountain Biking
Quantocks, Exmoor, Dartmoor

8 South East Mountain Biking
Ridgeway & Chilterns

9 South East Mountain Biking
North & South Downs

Available from bike shops, bookshops or direct from:

www.**v-outdoor**.co.uk